# AUTOHYPNOSIS

Here is a refreshingly well presented explanation of self-hypnosis based on recent advances in research into the unconscious mind. The author describes the mechanics of hypnosis and the benefits that can be derived from its use. He also provides step-by-step instructions on the safe use of self-hypnosis for non-medical purposes.

# AUTOHYPNOSIS
## A
# STEP-BY-STEP
# GUIDE TO
# SELF-HYPNOSIS

### RONALD SHONE
B.Sc., M.A.

THORSONS PUBLISHING GROUP

First published 1982
First published in this format 1987

British Library Cataloguing in Publication Data

Shone, R. (Ronald)
Autohypnosis: a step-by-guide
to self-hypnosis.
1. Autogenic training
I. Title
154.7'6      RC499.A8

ISBN 0-7225-1559-6

*Published by Thorsons Publishers Limited,
Wellingborough, Northamptonshire, NN8 2RQ, England*

Printed in Great Britain by
Richard Clay Limited, Bungay, Suffolk

4   6   8   10   9   7   5

# CONTENTS

# AN IMPORTANT NOTE

Since you should be aware of what you are intending to do, it is important that *before* you attempt any self-hypnosis you read through the whole of Part I. Put rather dramatically, it would be foolish to read about how to enter a hypnotic state and then go ahead and do so, without first knowing how to come out of it! Although you would eventually come out quite naturally, this may be after some unnecessary anxiety. All this means is that you should first learn some basic steps before you attempt to hypnotize yourself.

Part II can be read in any order, although the chapter on relaxation at the very least should be read and studied. Although all the different uses will not necessarily interest any particular individual, what you will gain by reading all the chapters is how to use a variety of techniques, and most particularly, how to improve your imagination. The rise of the imagination in sport is now becoming well recognized and a variety of books concerned with 'inner games' are now being published, some of which will be found in further reading. The vital point that I wish to stress here is the importance of developing your imagination and to use it in *all* hypnotic sessions and uses. Its application should not be confined to sport.

# INTRODUCTION

Autohypnosis, or self-hypnosis, means the hypnotizing of oneself. It is to be contrasted with heterohypnosis, which refers to the act of one person hypnotizing another person. Although, as we shall see later, all hypnosis is basically self-hypnosis, heterohypnosis and autohypnosis are not the same.

Hypnosis, as a phenomenon, is now becoming well documented and more readily accepted, but it is still clouded in mystery as far as the public at large is concerned. This arises partly out of sheer ignorance and partly from stage shows which still exist. But it need not be so. The question naturally arises: should everyone have access to this knowledge, or should it only be performed by 'experts'? Put in more practical terms: should hypnosis only be carried out by people in the medical profession? This is an important question to raise at this early stage because the answer will inevitably create an attitude of mind which is vital in reading this book – and, more importantly, carrying out the exercises. My brief answer to the question is that it should not be simply left to doctors. Why?

Consciousness, in all its manifestations, is concerned with our minds and how our body and mind interact. Hypnosis, as we shall see, concerns the unconscious mind – but still the mind of the hypnotized individual. Hypnosis is a 'natural' way of having access to the unconscious and, *if properly used*, is a means of achieving more of the potential which we all possess. The emphasis is undoubtedly on the phrase 'if properly used' because it is this which, it is argued, leads to dangers and so must be left to the experts. But this is taking things too far. If we employed this line of reasoning, then a car is dangerous because it can kill people. Therefore driving should only be done by 'experts'. We see from this analogy that it is not the car which is dangerous, but the person who drives (handles) the car dangerously. So too with hypnosis.

Hypnosis, whether autohypnosis or heterohypnosis, is not of itself dangerous, but it can become so in unscrupulous hands; this only refers to heterohypnosis because, generally speaking, people are not dangerous with themselves. The point is straightforward. Anything is dangerous if it is *deliberately* misused. The art is to know the tool and know how best to use it. Hypnosis is very simple and can be learnt very quickly by everyone. How to use it to its full potential is what takes time and practice.

This book is about hypnosis, more specifically self-hypnosis, and how to use it on oneself. Like any self-taught manual, it takes the reader step by step, with some detours into the psychology and physiology of what is taking place.

The present literature on hypnosis has a number of shortcomings. The first, and from our point of view the most important, is that most books contain poor descriptions of autohypnosis. Usually a text will limit itself to saying that you should first have it done to you by someone else. If this can be done, then all well and good. But for many people, this may be either impossible or undesirable.

Second, the texts are usually written by professional psychologists and psychiatrists. Their 'professionalism' demands the scientific approach with its experimentation which (a) can be replicated, and (b) is suitable and extensive enough to draw conclusions. However, the concentration on being 'scientific' usually means that the subjective experiences felt by individuals in these experiments either go under-recorded or not recorded at all. To the self-taught it is these subjective experiences which matter and which supply information that can be used for purposes of comparison.

Furthermore, to be told that seventy per cent of the population can be hypnotized (commonly quoted, although I would argue it is close on one hundred per cent) does not help a given individual. You want to know whether *you* can be hypnotized – and that is all that matters. It is the scientist who is interested in statistical tendencies. I shall state here, and again later, that everyone can be hypnotized – except for very young children and imbeciles. It may take time, it may require to be performed by the right person (in heterohypnosis) or by the right technique, (especially in autohypnosis), but it can and will succeed in all cases – eventually.

A third deficiency in the present literature is that authors do not explain why something may not have worked. There is a tendency to believe that when something does not work, then it never will. This is simply not true. Hypnotizability is not something you either have or you do not have. We all have it – but to different degrees. Realizing this, if a person fails to enter hypnosis, it is not simply because that person is not hypnotizable: there is some other reason. The problem, then, is what to do in such a case. Most texts give no instructions at this point.

A fourth short-coming is the inadequate emphasis on the role of the imagination in hypnosis. In man today, especially Western man, the imagination is very poorly developed. Our teaching methods develop logic and language (left brain functions), but not creativity and imagination (right brain functions). In this book we shall pay a great deal of attention to this. Many people fail in achieving autohypnosis, or sufficient depth in it, because they do not know how to use their imagination. We must learn how to redevelop the imagination: we must learn to utilize the right brain more fully.

In this book, no attempt will be made at supplying a history of hypnosis, not even a brief one. To drive a car does not require you to know the history of the automobile and, by the same token, to undertake self-hypnosis you do not need to know the history of hypnosis. Of course, history has its place and makes for interesting reading, and the reader will find a very readable and well documented introduction to such a history in Brian Inglis' *Natural and Supernatural*, which deals with the history of the paranormal from early times up to 1914. Nor will you find many references to particular authors. This is intended as an instruction manual. If you were repairing a car and following a set of instructions you would not break off to follow up what Joe Bloggs said in the Journal of ... My intention here is to supply a complete set of instructions which are self-contained. However, further reading is given at the end of the book.

The book is divided into two parts. Part I deals with the mechanics of self-hypnosis: what it is, how to enter it, how to deepen it, how to come out of it, etc. Part II is concerned with its non-medical uses. Self-hypnosis would not be very interesting, and certainly not worth the effort of learning, if there was little you could do with it. The stimulus to write this book comes partly from recent advances into the unconscious mind, and partly from the non-medical uses to which you yourself can put this technique—once it is learnt. There are now a variety of texts listing the medical uses of hypnosis, some of which will be found in the further reading section, but very few works exist on the non-medical uses of hypnosis.

One use stands out above all others, however, and that is as a means of achieving relaxation. Even if hypnosis were used for no other purpose than this, it would be worth the investment of time. But there are many methods of relaxation. Hypnosis has the advantage that it achieves this quickly *and* can be used for a variety of other things. It is the manifold uses of hypnosis which make it such a useful technique to know.

Hypnosis, whether autohypnosis or heterohypnosis, is no panacea. Nor is it a means of becoming superhuman. It is simply a method of reaching your unconscious mind and marshalling the energy force which is present; a force which most of us fail to tap, thus preventing us from attaining our full potential. Hypnosis will not enable you to do something that you cannot do; it can, however, allow you to go beyond what you normally do, because it allows you to tap your reserves of energy which are there for you to call on—if you knew but how.

# PART I

## SELF-HYPNOSIS:
## HOW AND WHY IT WORKS

# 1
# SOME PRELIMINARY
# CONSIDERATIONS

This first chapter will discuss what is meant by hypnosis and draw a distinction between autohypnosis and heterohypnosis. In doing this, I shall draw on recent research into right and left brain consciousness, which contributes more to our understanding of hypnosis (besides a variety of other aspects of the mind), than anything in the whole history of the subject. These aspects will be examined throughout the book and developed in appropriate places. I shall deal here with any possible dangers which may be thought to exist, and also discuss the typical types of worries people have about hypnosis. Finally, in this chapter, consideration will be given to the frame of mind that you should adopt, both in your reading and in the practice sessions. This is paramount and could very well determine your success or failure. I would argue, however, that there cannot be failure: there are only degrees of success. Everyone can play tennis, but some people are better than others. We can all, however, get satisfaction from the degree of our success – so long as we are reaching our full potential.

## Can We Define Hypnosis?
Hypnosis is a particular state of mind. It is known to exist, but at present this state of consciousness is not fully defined. For

this reason, hypnosis is usually described in terms of the characteristics which are associated with it. But this is fairly meaningless until you yourself have experienced the state. It is not my aim to define hypnosis here, but I shall talk around it so that you have some idea about the state of mind I am talking about.

In coming to an understanding of hypnosis, therefore, it is first useful to consider two other states of mind: namely, being awake and being asleep. Now we are all aware that we are not awake one minute and asleep the next. Furthermore, we know from our own experience that we are more or less awake at different times of the day. In other words, our consciousness, or awareness, varies continuously. Even our sleep varies in depth, as can be detected by means of an electroencephalograph (EEG). But we know this ourselves from the experience of awakening and having moments (which occasionally can last some time) of being 'half awake and half asleep'. This same state of mind can occur when we are sitting in a chair in front of a warm fire, or even when watching TV.

The point we are establishing is a simple, but important, one. There exists a continuum between being completely awake (fully conscious) and being deeply asleep (non-awareness). Hypnosis, in being a state of mind, exists along part of this continuum. A hypnotized person is fully awake, as shown by EEG brain wave patterns, yet has some outward appearances of being asleep. But in actual fact, hypnosis and sleep are quite different. The similarity is purely superficial – and although the word 'hypnosis' is from the Greek meaning sleep, this is purely historical. Even so, as we shall see, the association of sleep with certain bodily changes is often utilized in hypnotic routines.

Ever since Freud, we have distinguished between the conscious mind and the unconscious mind. Up until about 1965, however, very few people would have suggested that these are located in any specific parts of the brain – the exceptions being researches into Eastern and mystic philosophies. Now there is growing evidence that the conscious mind, as generally understood, is located in the left hemisphere of the brain, while the unconscious mind is located in the right hemisphere. Figure 1 illustrates that the brain is composed of two halves, which we shall refer to as the 'right brain' and the 'left brain'. We now know that these have very different attributes, i.e. functions (see Figure 1). It is not my intention here to go into these new and fascinating discoveries; all I wish to do is to concentrate on those features which are important in coming to an understanding of hypnosis and how to use it.

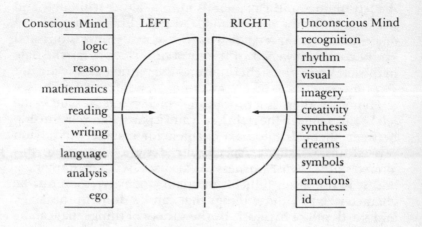

| Conscious Mind | LEFT | RIGHT | Unconscious Mind |
|---|---|---|---|
| logic | | | recognition |
| reason | | | rhythm |
| mathematics | | | visual |
| reading | | | imagery |
| writing | | | creativity |
| language | | | synthesis |
| analysis | | | dreams |
| ego | | | symbols |
| | | | emotions |
| | | | id |

Figure 1.

The unconscious mind (composing the id in Freudian psychology) works according to the *pleasure principle*, i.e. it avoids pain and obtains pleasure, regardless of external considerations. Important, from our point of view, is that the pains and pleasures are composed of emotions which manifest themselves *now*. Emotions can only exist *now*; there is no such thing as a future emotion. You can have an emotion now about something in the future, but the emotion you feel occurs now. In addition, you cannot think about an emotion without feeling it, without experiencing it, a point we shall return to later.

The conscious mind (composing the ego) works according to the *reality principle*, i.e. images are tested against reality and, if necessary, bodily tensions are delayed until the appropriate environmental conditions are obtained. Thus, the ego is realistic and logical, and its purpose is to create a plan which can be executed in the environment in which the individual lives, in order to achieve its satisfaction. Put briefly, the id requires immediate satisfaction while the ego intervenes and chooses the time, the place, and which emotions are to be satisfied. The ego is the executor of the id.

From the figure on page 13, it is obvious that words occur in the left brain – in the conscious mind – along with logic and reasoning. On the other hand, the right brain is the seat of emotions and imagery, of rhythm, visual impressions and synthesis. When we talk of 'a state of mind', we mean the state of the left brain, the right brain and the particular way the two sides interact.

Hypnosis, then, is a procedure which creates a state in the left brain, a state in the right brain and a particular relationship between them. In the next chapter, for instance, induction procedures which are specifically designed to create this altered state of consciousness will be discussed. Once attained, and it is not at all difficult to attain, then hypnosis can be characterized by those things that can be done in this state, and the depth of hypnosis by the variety of things that can be done when in such a state. It should not surprise the reader to find that there is a dispute over what characteristics are associated with the hypnotic state, and how to measure the depth. But this is of academic interest. An analysis of left and right brains will aid understanding of this point, but more importantly, it will help in overcoming any difficulties *you* may have in achieving the hypnotic state.

As long ago as 1605, Francis Bacon in *The Advancement of Learning* pointed out that some things can only be learned by experiencing them. A child cannot understand the meaning of being burnt if it has never experienced this sensation. A person can read and hear about love, but cannot understand it until it has been experienced – until the emotion has been felt. If you consider this in the light of right and left brain functions, we see that some things we can learn by means of words and logic because they are purely left brain functions. But other things such as sensations, emotions, imagery and rhythm are all right brain functions, and these must be experienced. No amount of repetition using words can create the experience of rhythm – this must be experienced subjectively by you and you alone.

Once an emotion has been experienced, then reading about it can give more meaning to it. But this meaning comes from relating the information read, which is experienced by the left brain, to the emotion, which has been experienced by the right brain. This is crucial to understanding hypnosis and is worth discussing further.

Between the right and left hemispheres of the brain there exists a bundle of nerves called the corpus callosum. In the past it was thought that this did not have any major function, but this simply reflected our ignorance. The corpus callosum acts like a barrier between the right and left brains (knowledge of this was obtained when the corpus callosum was cut to prevent seizures in epileptic patients).

From what has been said so far, the corpus callosum must act like a barrier because if it did not, every word thought would create a host of emotions and, conversely, each emotion would create a torrent of words. In the majority of cases each word we see, speak or hear does not generate emotions. It is as if they enter the left brain and stay there. This makes sense. If you are reading a novel, the words are 'processed' in the left brain: there is no reason to involve your right brain. Similarly, you can feel some emotion totally and absolutely and it need never be expressed by means of words – and some of our deepest emotions are 'expressionless'.

Of course, a word may generate an emotion or an emotion may generate the word by which we designate it. In this case the barrier is breached. This is shown schematically in Figure 2, but at the moment we do not know how this process works. What is important, from our present point of view, is that when using hypnosis we reach the right brain (the unconscious mind) by means of words (the use of the conscious mind). The process of hypnosis, more specifically, hypnotic induction, is a means of achieving a fairly easy pathway from the left brain (the conscious) to the right brain (the unconscious). Once this bridge is formed the hypnotic state can be deepened and utilized.

Before finishing this section, it is important to point out that

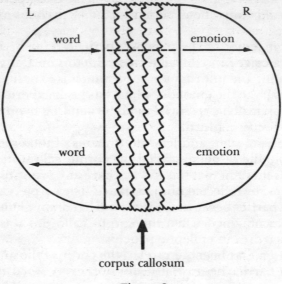

Figure 2.

we have all almost certainly experienced brief periods of the
hypnotic state, but may not have been aware of it. A few
examples will illustrate this. Have you ever been reading and,
just on turning over the page, realized that you cannot
remember anything of the page you have just 'read'? Have you
experienced that drive on the motorway where some 30 miles
have gone by without your being aware of it? Have you ever
stood at a bus-stop waiting, and what seems like fifteen or
thirty minutes have gone by when it has, in fact, been only
two? Or the converse, when you have been so absorbed in
something that hours have passed and you have imagined it
was some thirty minutes? Have you gone into a chemist and,
before you are aware of it, a 'jingle' about brand x is going
through your mind? Have you ever been so absorbed in a
book or film that you have been oblivious to your surroundings?

All of these have features common with the hypnotic state.
The major difference is that they are isolated events and other
things soon impinge on your consciousness to terminate
them. What is important is that they do occur, you do

experience them, and they are not psychological abnormalities – otherwise, we would all be abnormal! With some learning, it is possible to consciously create the conditions in which these states may occur and be maintained. In other words, there is nothing particularly 'magical' about the hypnotic state.

## Dangers

The obvious question to raise at this point is whether there are any dangers in undertaking such a venture. If self-hypnosis is gone about in the right way, there are none. This may seem like a bold statement to make, but it is justified. The reason lies in what we said at the end of the last section. Hypnosis is a state of mind which has been experienced, at one time or another, by everyone. The ability and the mechanics of achieving the hypnotic state are already within us. It is simply a question of unlocking the secret. Of course, if hypnosis is not handled correctly, then dangers can occur.

The essential danger of hypnosis, particularly self-hypnosis, is using it as a method of undertaking psychoanalysis, whether intentionally or unintentionally. Hypnosis is quite distinct from psychoanalysis, but it is used by psychoanalysts, (in which case it is referred to as hypnotherapy) because it is an expedient and drug-free method of reaching the unconscious mind. The danger is not with hypnosis as such, but with the disclosure of some feature of the personality that a person may not wish to know about. The mind has developed a technique of repressing hurtful experiences, especially those of childhood, and it is almost certain that these are housed in the right brain. If hypnosis is combined with a probing into a person's personality, then it is here that the danger lies. *This should not be done without the direction of a professional psychoanalyst or psychiatrist.*

One other difficulty is worth mentioning. This is not so much a danger as a problem of how to deal with the unexpected. The danger is in not knowing what to do or how to respond to the unexpected. Happily, these are few in number. Take a simple case where a person has been hypnotized and, for no apparent reason, begins to sob. If this was a heterohypnotic session, i.e. involving a hypnotist and a person being hypnotized who is presently sobbing, then the hypnotist has basically two courses of action. Either he may begin by asking the hypnotized person why he is sobbing; or he may suggest to the subject that there is no reason to sob, that everything is all right, etc. – if necessary, change the scene by suggesting to the person that he is somewhere very pleasant. The first approach, however, is very close to psycho-analysis. These two approaches are open in self-hypnosis. But, in this instance, you either know why you are sobbing or you don't. If you do not, then asking for explanations may not be sensible. Persistent repetition that there is no reason to sob, is all that is necessary.

The same applies if you do not come out of hypnosis on termination. This is far more likely to occur in heterohypnosis than self-hypnosis, although, even in the former case, it is rare. If it does occur, however, all one needs to do is to repeat the termination suggestion. Not coming out of hypnosis when instructed to do so, arises not because something dangerous has occurred. On the contrary, the most usual reason is because the hypnotized person finds the state so thoroughly relaxing and beneficial to the body that he wishes to prolong the state.

But there is one other reason, which is not beneficial, and deserves attention. It may be that some earlier suggestion which was given, even if given by yourself, has not been cancelled. Take a simple example. Suppose you had suggested to yourself, while under hypnosis, that your right arm will be numb. Suppose you were very successful in achieving this. Let us further suppose that you now attempt to awaken yourself without cancelling the feeling of numbness. It may well be the case that you will not awaken. And the reason why you may not awaken is that your unconscious mind knows that you have not cancelled the feeling of numbness, and that if you awaken it will be troublesome – the unconscious mind is very clever and always acts in your best interests. The lesson to learn from this is that you should *always cancel or nullify any suggestion that you do not wish to take effect in the waking state*.

One final side-effect is worth commenting on. Some people, although not many, find that when they awaken they have a slight headache – usually caused by the level of concentration. However, this soon goes. Even so, there is no need for it to occur in the first place. The termination suggestion which is outlined in Chapter 2, incorporates a statement that you will awaken feeling fine, relaxed, fresh and alert. In this way you use suggestion to eliminate any possibility of a headache. Even if you do not suffer from any headache, as the majority find, it is always useful to terminate a session with suggestions of awakening feeling fine, relaxed, fresh and alert.

## Other Concerns About Being Hypnotized

Having eased your mind that there are no dangers in the use of hypnosis, if properly executed, and not becoming alarmed when the unexpected happens, other questions often spring to mind. These may include: Will I become unconscious? Will I be able to wake up in an emergency or if the door bell or telephone rings? Does it mean that I am weak-willed if I can be hypnotized? If I am hypnotizable, does it mean that I am gullible? Will I do everything that the hypnotist says, and so be 'under his power'? These are just some of the usual worries, and although they apply largely to heterohypnosis they are worth commenting on because of the light that they shed on the hypnotic state, and also because of their meaninglessness when directed at the state of self-hypnosis – a point so often overlooked. In the remainder of this section we shall deal with some of these concerns; others will be dealt with elsewhere, once the hypnotic technique has been described.

## Loss of Consciousness

This is by far the greatest worry, largely because people feel they may be indiscreet and not be aware of it. The essence of this general misconception is the idea that when you become hypnotized you 'blank out', as in sleep; that you become unaware of anything that you are doing. If this was truly the case, then if the hypnotist gave you suggestions you would not consciously 'hear' them and so nothing would happen. We do not usually respond to suggestions during hours of sleep or when unconscious, say from a blow on the head. On the contrary, when you are hypnotized, you are usually super-alert, far more than in your normal waking state.

As we shall see later, when you become hypnotized your left brain 'goes to sleep' – by this I mean it is largely bypassed, and when a part of the brain is not used it 'shuts itself down' or 'goes to sleep'. Now, when hypnotized, most of your left brain is not operating and words become focused (i.e. concentrated) just like a beam of light which is focused on a point by a lens. This allows the words to penetrate through the corpus callosum and into the right brain, which is now more fully brought into operation. By shutting down the conscious brain you (a) stop the reality principle from operating, and (b) allow the words to penetrate the corpus callosum and create images and emotions which satisfy the pleasure principle. In all this you are fully aware of what is going on – more aware than when fully awake.

There is one exception which is important to mention and that is a somnambulist. Somnambulism is the deepest state of hypnosis in which a person carries out all suggestions, but is usually unaware of doing so. Now how do we explain this phenomenon? The point is that the left brain *totally* 'goes to sleep' and for such persons, words pass directly through the corpus callosum and into the right brain where they are acted upon – usually very literally. Only about five per cent of the population can achieve a somnambulistic state. With regard to self-hypnosis, this will seldom occur because in such a state you become incapable of giving yourself any further suggestions. If it does occur, then you will literally fall asleep and awaken in your own good time– as you would if you fell asleep in the chair while watching TV.

Why some people are somnambulistic is not known. To achieve this state can be very relaxing and most beneficial, and is very like the state of *Samadhi* referred to in Eastern mysticism. It is interesting to note that, in the East, elaborate exercises are set up in the hope of achieving Samadhi, the state of super-consciousness, while in the West, man is generally afraid of losing his state of consciousness, his reason. The West is left brain dominated while the East is right brain dominated. What is required is a suitable blend of the two, with full knowledge of what is happening. At the present stage of man's development, we can only achieve partial understanding.

## Weak-willed and Gullible
Some people believe that if you can be hypnotized it is a sign that you are weak-willed and gullible. The misconception in

this belief is the assumption that the person being hypnotized surrenders his will to that of the hypnotist. (Of course those who believe this have difficulty in comprehending self-hypnosis!) It is very important to realize that a hypnotized person still thinks, and thinks logically, (but with a type of logic that is referred to as trance logic, which will be explained later); he can still make decisions, and will only do what is not against his or her moral code. The reason for this is that a hypnotized person does not lose contact with reality altogether – how else could he carry out some of the things suggested. And if one accepts the Freudian classification of personality, consisting of the id, the ego and the super-ego (the last embracing a person's values and morals), then it would appear that, during hypnosis, the super-ego is not affected either. Unfortunately, this does not mean that a person in hetero-hypnosis cannot be made to do something they normally would not, because they can be 'tricked' into believing they are doing something which is not against their moral code. Under self-hypnosis this is absolutely impossible.

We now know from experience that strong-willed people are often more readily hypnotizable than the reverse situation. This hints at an essential ingredient in hypnosis, which is also important for people engaging in self-hypnosis. The crux of the matter is whether a person wishes to use his will to co-operate with the hypnotist or against the hypnotist. This can also be explained by means of Figure 2 on page 16, showing the corpus callosum or barrier between the left and right brains. It seems reasonable to hypothesize that if the will is used to co-operate with the hypnotist then will-power is used to help cross the bridge between the two brains, first in one direction and then in the other. However, if the will is used against the suggestions, then in all likelihood the bridge will not be crossed and the person will not be hypnotized. The stronger the will, the more successful the hypnosis is, when used in co-operation, but the more unsuccessful it is when the will is used against the hypnotic process. Thus, statements like: 'I'm too strong-willed to be hypnotized', indicate a total misconception about hypnosis. In the hypnotic induction and deepening, the will can be used either to co-operate or to hinder. The same applies to self-hypnosis. It is important that for success your will is co-operating and not hindering.

What about being gullible, i.e. believing anything you are told? Again, it is not necessarily true that those who are gullible are 'natural' hypnotic subjects, or that if you are hypnotizable you are therefore gullible. Hypnosis is a state of mind, and since hypnosis does not, in any way, impair your decision-making abilities, you are as gullible in the hypnotic state as you are in your waking state.

What messages can we draw from these observations that will be of help for the person who wishes to engage in self-hypnosis? First, you must have the co-operation of your will. If you wish to succeed, it is no good giving yourself suggestions and mentally trying hard to prevent them from working. This is certainly a temptation in hypnosis because it is used as a means of 'proof' of being hypnotized. Far from being proof, it will simply make it difficult or impossible to achieve the hypnotic state. When you learn a sport or learn to play a musical instrument, you learn the instructions and follow them to the best of your ability. You do not hinder the learning by deliberately not co-operating. We see, then, that you must want it to happen and expect it to happen. We shall say more on this later. Second, like any learning process you must apply yourself to the task and bring to bear your conscious attention. Studies have shown that the more motivated you are, the more you are likely to succeed. The belief, whole-hearted belief, that something will occur is a tremendous force in achieving success. This is a message taught by many mystics, not least Christ.

## Who is Hypnotizable?

In books on hypnosis, a fair amount of attention is paid to a consideration of who in the population is hypnotizable. Of course, the reader may find this interesting, but the overriding question is: 'Am I hypnotizable?' and, more to the point in our present context, 'Can I hypnotize myself?' What I intend to do in this section, is to point out that everyone can be hypnotized. But more importantly, from your perspective, is to draw from these investigations useful information about the hypnotic process which will be invaluable in learning self-hypnosis.

The information available, indicates that about seventy per cent of the population can be hypnotized. If, for a moment, we assume that this applies to a given hypnotist, then a different hypnotist may also lead to seventy per cent of the population being hypnotized – but they will be a *different* set of people (there will, of course, be some overlap, but what matters is that the second group contains persons who were not in the first group). Change the hypnotist enough times and eventually everyone will be accounted for. We have not even talked about technique. Part of the reason why a particular person does not become hypnotized is not because he is not hypnotizable, but rather because the induction technique does not suit him.

The conclusions we draw from this are that a person may not be hypnotized by one hypnotist, but may be by another (using the same technique), or that a person may not be hypnotized by one technique, but is by another (using the same hypnotist). It is my contention that everyone can be hypnotized – with the exception of very young children and imbeciles. Very young children have not sufficiently developed word sense in their left brains to begin the process. Imbeciles cannot retain information in their left brains long enough for it to even begin to break through the barrier formed by the corpus callosum. In the second case, the missing ingredients are attention and concentraton, both of which are necessary for a hypnotic state to be induced.

Now the reasons why a particular person is not hypnotizable by a particular hypnotist are varied. It may be that the hypnotist is of the same (or opposite) sex; that they smoke; that they are domineering; that they remind the person of their mother, father, husband, etc. These and many more factors have been recorded. They all boil down, however, to the lack of rapport between the subject and the hypnotist. Now this may be true of heterohypnosis, but it cannot be true of autohypnosis – unless you do really dislike your inner self! The important question of rapport is only meaningful in the case of heterohypnosis. But in the case of self-hypnosis a greater burden is placed on the self. Rapport can be taken to mean trust in the hypnotist and a willingness to place this trust and confidence in him. In self-hypnosis this has to be directed at yourself. What it means is that you must have confidence in yourself and a confidence that you will succeed. This is absolutely essential. You must believe in it absolutely. If your basic problem is lack of confidence in yourself, and this may be a reason why you wish to learn self-hypnosis, then you must try hard to believe absolutely that you can and will succeed in hypnotizing yourself – and not only that you will succeed, but that you will be very successful indeed. Methods for raising your general self-confidence are dealt with in Chapter 9.

In gaining this confidence, you must begin with experiences that you have had already which have characteristics of the hypnotic state. I - will now discuss some of these and, in particular, draw attention to the left-right brain features of them. This discussion will also supply information as to why, for a particular person, one technique may fail, while another will succeed – whether in heterohypnosis or self-hypnosis.

First let us consider what happens when you become very absorbed in something, such as a book or a film. Studies show that those people who, when they read, become deeply involved and relate in some way to the characters are usually good hypnotic subjects. Some people relate directly with the hero or heroine and 'become that person'; others become an observer to the scene which is unfolding. The same applies in films. Now if you consider this for a moment you will realize that such individuals are reading with both sides of their brain and not simply the left brain. This can readily be grasped if the same people read a very technical report, because this is done almost wholly with the left brain.

The observation to make from this type of involvement is the act of 'suppressing your own identity'. When you become Don Quixote or Helen of Troy you identify with these persons. If you identify directly then you may feel what they feel; if you are an observer you may have certain emotions, depending on your response to what is happening in the scene that you are observing. In both cases, you involve the right brain; involvement cannot be achieved with the left brain alone. The more you can identify with the hero or heroine, the more the right brain is included in the reading or watching operation, and the more of the left brain is 'switched off'. It is not unknown to be quite oblivious to everything going on around you because you have 'switched off' your hearing and focused all your attention on the scene being created by the novel or film. Another way of considering such involvement is that for this period you suspend reality. This should be clear. Reality-testing is a left brain function and you are clearly not Don Quixote or Helen of Troy, as your left brain will readily tell you. But reading and watching a film is much more pleasurable if you suspend such reality-testing – and obviously so, because you are then allowing the pleasure principle of the right brain to become operative.

The arts are, of course, ideal for cultivating such involvement. Education in the West is extremely left brain dominated. If you look back at Figure 1 on page 13 and think back to your school days, it is pretty clear that something like ninety per cent or more of your time was directed at developing left brain functions. A muscle that goes unused becomes flabby and loses its ability to function effectively. The same applies to the nerves. Your right brain has had very little *conscious* exercise. This may mean that the type of involvement we have discussed so far is something that you have not experienced before. What then can you do?

You must discover amongst all the things that you do, something in which you are able to 'lose yourself'. It may be sport, it may be playing a musical instrument, fishing, or simply observing the clouds moving across the sky. Whatever it is, the important point is to establish when it does happen and consciously think about those circumstances – apply both your right and your left brain in the experience. Notice your feelings. When you engage in autohypnosis you can only draw on your own experiences because it is purely subjective. The more atrophied your right brain is from misuse, then the smaller number of such experiences you can probably call on. Turn to art. By this, I do not necessarily mean take up painting or stand for hours looking at Picasso's, wondering if they have any significance whatsoever. What I do mean is cultivate hobbies or take note of things that supply sustenance to the right brain. Music is an excellent beginning, and classical music in particular. Find any that you like, regardless of the composer. Take up dancing, of any kind, since this will improve rhythm; handiwork or handicraft, which improves form and shape along with creativity – anything that stimulates the right brain into action.

It is well documented that people in the forces, nurses, teachers and students tend, on average, to be good hypnotic subjects. Now what is important, from our point of view, is that not all these people have the involvement that we have just discussed. This implies that they must possess some other attribute which leads to success in hypnosis. The question is 'What attribute is it?' The basic attribute is the *willingness* to accept instructions. This in no way means they are zombies or automatons; it simply means that, *in certain situations*, they are willing to accept instructions in an uncritical manner – which of course gives their actions the characteristic of being automatic. The forces and nursing are clearly based on such a premise. It by no means follows that such people are uncritical; they can be most critical and vociferous. It is simply that, in certain situations, they are willing to suspend criticism and follow the instructions.

Teaching is also based on this idea; the willingness, up to a point, to accept the word of someone in authority – 'the expert'. You are willing to 'play along', as it were, on the assumption that you will gain something or learn something by so doing. The academic often says that he takes a critical stand. This is nonsense, or at least only partially true. If it were true, he would never progress past saying 'I'. He readily accepts some instructions and, when appropriate, is critical in other situations. The student for most of the time is listening to instructions and is uncritical. He will tend to put on his critical cap when he has to write an essay.

This is no different from learning a sport or learning to play the piano. In the first instance you must learn the 'rules of the game' and, when doing this, you will tend to accept instructions and follow them uncritically. The footballer is told that the object of the game is to kick the ball in the opponents' net. If you asked why, the only answer that could be given is that that is the object of the game. However, when a coach is instructing a routine, it is right and proper to ask why. If the answer is accepted, the footballer then takes an uncritical attitude and places all his attention and concentration on the instructions. When learning to play the piano, you are given instructions in playing scales. You do not ask: 'Why should I?' because you know that these are necessary if you wish (if you are willing) to learn to play the piano. Notice that you must be motivated and want to play the piano – it is the youngster who is not motivated and does not want to play who raises hell and expostulates: 'Why should I?'!

The same is basically true when learning hypnosis. You should adopt, *during the process*, a willingness to follow instructions uncritically – to 'play the game'. If you say to yourself: 'Why should I?' or 'That makes no sense'., then you activate the critical faculties in the left brain and so make the hypnotic induction ineffective. Basically, you have approached hypnosis with a negative attitude, which indicates a lack of motivation. Of course, this does not mean that you should be uncritical *outside* of the hypnotic session, and it is fitting that outside you are critical. In fact, this whole chapter is supplying answers to those likely critical questions you will probably ask.

An uncritical willingness to accept instructions has two features which are important if hypnosis is to succeed. We have pointed out already that reality-testing takes place in the left brain. This means that any new information from the senses is compared with stored, pre-existing, accumulated information you have in your mind. If there is no inconsistency, then the mind, (strictly in this case the left brain) accepts it as reality. Take the following illustration: Suppose I place before you a rose in a vase, but I say that it is a Christmas tree. You now have conflicting sensory information. In all likelihood you will reject what I said and believe what you see. However, if the left brain is not operative, or not fully operative, and reality-testing is suspended, then the object before you, if positioned in your *left* field of vision, *is* a Christmas tree since you have no reality to compare it with; the reality is what you see and what the object is called *at that particular moment.*

Let us take this a little further by considering, for a moment, dreams. A look back at Figure 1 on page 13 will indicate that dreaming is a right brain activity. It has been known for a long time that dreams can supply information about the unconscious mind. We all dream, but some people are better at remembering them than others. To remember a dream means to bring it into conscious awareness. This, in turn, means that the content of a dream must pass from the right brain to the left brain. Again, the reason why dreams are difficult to remember probably has something to do with the function of the corpus callosum.

When you dream, things are 'real' as far as your emotions and reactions are concerned. Because you dream when you are asleep, your body is restricted in what responses it can make. It is usually restricted to heart beat, perspiration and breathing (those things controlled by the autonomic nervous system). Even the bizarre, symbolic dream, often with impossible things happening together, appear to have their own internal logic: the dream appears consistent within its own framework.

The point I am making is that dreams do not use the reality of the left brain, nor do they use the logic and reasoning of the left brain. Dreams are a feature of the right brain and use largely symbols, emotions and synthesis as a mode of expression. Different things occur in the same scene because they reinforce each other to convey an impression – or even a message. The point I wish to stress is that, insofar as hypnosis is concerned with the right brain and suspends reality-testing, then the reality is what is created in the right brain at that moment of time. The reality *is* what is suggested to the person at that moment of time. Unlike sleep, however, the body is fully functional and can and will respond to the reality so suggested. This explains, for example, the typical show routine of suggesting to a hypnotized person that he is, say, a cat. If he is a good subject and reality-testing has been sufficiently repressed, then the person will behave like a cat. Such a person knows that he is not a cat, but this information is stored in the left brain which is, temporarily, 'asleep'. The person's reality at that moment is only what is contained in the suggestion and how the person wishes to interpret this suggestion. Responses differ, depending on how the information is interpreted by the hypnotized person.

Now, if you consider this unreasonable, let me just explain a typical experiment done on split brain patients. These are individuals who have had their corpus callosum cut, so that their brains literally are in two halves. The experiment is illustrated in Figure 3. The individual is asked to stare at a spot in the centre of the screen. Then a word or picture is flashed on to, say, the left side of the screen. Because vision is reversed on entering the brain, this word or picture will be seen only by the right brain. If the subject is asked what he saw, information that goes to his left brain, he is unable to say— he may of course guess, but this is not allowed. But if the individual is allowed to feel the objects on the table with his left hand, which is connected to his right brain, then the object indicated on the screen can be recognized from the group of objects. Thus, if a nude woman is flashed on the left of the screen, (and seen by the right brain), he may blush, and if asked why he is blushing, (information taken in by his left brain), he is unable to give you the reason. And so too with hypnosis. A suggestion is taken up by the right brain and acted on, if the reality-testing of the left brain is suppressed. The individual is awake, in the usual sense of the word, but will respond to the 'reality' which has been suggested in the right brain.

As pointed out earlier, the individual who is hypnotized can still make decisions and still has a moral code, but these are now in relation to the 'reality' suggested. Now in self hypnosis there cannot be a complete break between the two halves, because it is the left brain which uses words in the form of suggestions to make contact with the right brain. The more the left brain, however, can be 'put to sleep', the more successful will be your self-hypnosis.

## Summary of the Attitudes You Should Adopt

What, then, are the attitudes you should adopt when you do self-hypnosis? There are basically four attitudes:

1. You must be *motivated*. You must want to be hypnotized, (either by means of someone else or by yourself), and you must want to succeed at it. Beginning the endeavour half-heartedly is not a ticket to success. You must want to succeed and believe that you will succeed.

2. You must be *involved* in the process. Hypnosis is not, as many believe, a passive act. It requires your full involvement and positive participation. In other words, you must apply yourself, direct your attention and concentrate on the process.

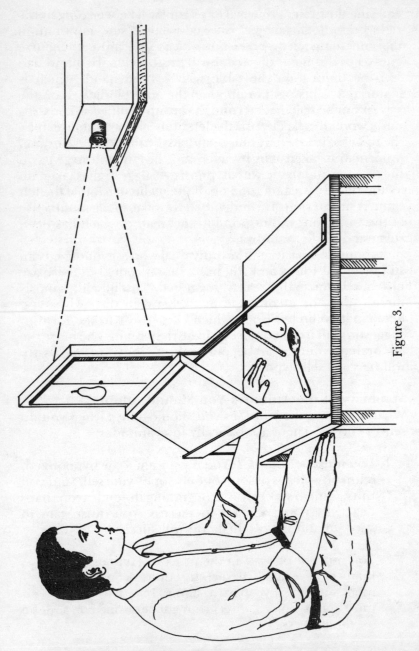

Figure 3.

3. You must direct your *will to co-operate* and not to go against the hypnotic process. This is not the same as wanting something to happen. You may want something to happen, but apply your will negatively, so that it is difficult or impossible for it to happen.

4. You must approach hypnosis with an *uncritical acceptance,* at least during the practice sessions. Only by doing this will you allow suggestions to pass from your left brain into your right brain.

No one of these is absolutely necessary – in the sense that if one is absent then hypnosis is impossible. Nor do you require all of them to be present simultaneously. However, the more you can develop these attributes the more successful you will be. It is not a question of either having these attributes or not, as the case may be, but rather to what degree you have them. Furthermore, now that they have been highlighted, it is a question of how you can increase their effectiveness. Half the battle is knowing what they are and how to recognize them. Now that you have done this, it only remains for later chapters to show you how you can improve them and constantly improve your self-hypnosis. Even for those who have already attempted self-hypnosis, the information contained in this chapter and later chapters will show how it can be deepened.

# 2
# INDUCTION AND
# TERMINATION

In this chapter, just two of the most important aspects of hypnosis will be considered: its induction and how to terminate the state. I shall also refer to some useful points about giving yourself suggestions. This is necessary because some suggestions you will respond to, while others may be ineffective. Some general ideas about suggestions will help to make them more effective. In the final section, I shall consider the question, 'How do I know that I am hypnotized?'

One preliminary comment is worth making, and concerns all suggestions (instructions) given in this book. Although we shall give induction and termination instructions in detail, you do not need to keep to these. You can devise your own. In the first instance, however, it is best to try the ones given here. This is not unreasonable. If you are learning to play the piano, you first learn from already composed pieces of music. When these are mastered and understood, then you can improvize. So too with hypnosis.

## Induction
Induction means the process by which the hypnotic state is achieved. Although some people enter this state fairly readily, in general it must be learnt. Hypnosis is a purely subjective

experience and only you can do it. Whether you are being hypnotized by someone else or by yourself, it is *you* who must alter your state of consciousness. It is very much like learning to ride a bicycle. The first problem to overcome in learning to ride a bicycle is having confidence in yourself and convincing yourself that, although you will be on only two wheels which are only a few inches wide, with enough momentum, you will stay upright. So too with hypnosis. Once the state has been achieved and experienced, it can be repeated very easily and will become easier on each future occasion. Furthermore, with each practice you will become more proficient, just as in any other learning process. Once learnt, it is not forgotten – but without practice you can become rusty.

Before we set out the instructions in detail, it will be worth commenting on what is being done. All induction procedures are specifically designed to reach the right brain, the unconscious mind. In order to do this, the left brain must be 'put to sleep' as much as possible. In heterohypnosis, access to the right brain is often accomplished by giving the left brain a mental task so as to keep it occupied.

A typical illustration is when a hypnotist asks a subject to mentally count backwards from three hundred and to continue this while the hypnotist talks. Thus, the left brain is kept occupied while the hypnotist's suggestions are picked up and passed on to the right brain. Notice, in particular, that the suggestions being given by the hypnotist cannot be assessed in any critical manner. This is because you cannot pay attention to two things simultaneously. You can switch between them, but at any moment of time only one is the focus of your attention. But having understood this, there is a problem for the person engaged in self-hypnosis: they cannot perform it. So we must adapt the technique slightly.

A second operation is being carried out during the induction stage. Specifically, it is the quietening of the mind. A quiet mind is more responsive to suggestions. This is very important to understand, especially for the self-hypnotist. In this day and age, with its many pressures and anxieties, this is easier said than done. Let me, then, explain what is happening as the mind is being quietened. The mind responds to stimuli which come through the senses: touch, taste, smell, sight and hearing. The idea is to reduce these to an absolute minimum. As the mind has less to occupy it, it focuses more and more on those stimuli which it is still receiving. We shall develop this more as the chapter progresses.

What it does reveal, however, is that the first thing you must do when you intend to hypnotize yourself is to find a quiet place. You should either sit with your back straight or lie down. There should not be too much light, especially on the first few occasions. Neither should there by any draughts and you should not be feeling cold. One other point, sometimes overlooked, is that you should ensure that you go to the toilet before you begin. Having got into this comfortable position, the induction procedure can begin. It usually begins by getting you to close your eyes – as I shall demonstrate in a moment. For the present, it is important to understand why. Sight involves a great deal of information, which is processed by both sides of the brain, and so the sooner the eyes are closed, the quicker such information is cut off and the sooner the mind can be quietened.

You are now in a particularly interesting state. If you are being hypnotized by someone else, then basically you only have two sources of information: the suggestions of the hypnotist and your own internal bodily sensations. Now the mind is a curious thing. When it has no *outside* stimuli to process then it will turn to *internal* sensations. This is the very thing that the hypnotist wants. If you are hypnotizing yourself, then *all* stimuli are internal.

The next stage of the induction process is to get the mind to think about bodily sensations – something most of us do very rarely. At the same time, a gradual process of putting the left brain to 'sleep' is undertaken. If you just close your eyes for a few moments, you will soon realize that all sorts of thoughts begin to impinge on your consciousness. Slowly but surely, these are reduced, and attention is directed to specific bodily sensations. As your mind quietens, that is as more and more of your left brain 'shuts down', it becomes easier to concentrate on the one thing and keep your attention on it. Notice in all this, how willingness and co-operation are essential. Also notice that it is through suggestion that all these changes are being brought about. At this stage you will be in a light hypnotic trance. Also, you should be feeling very relaxed – but I will discuss bodily sensations in more detail in Chapter 4.

It should be apparent that what is happening is a shutting down of parts of the left brain, so as to direct the thoughts on to the suggestions alone. This allows the suggestions to penetrate the corpus callosum and into the right brain. An analogy will help: If you take a lens, light will hit it and pass through in rather a dispersed fashion. If, however, the lens is angled correctly, then the light can be concentrated on a point. The process of hypnosis is like the lens, it concentrates the suggestions, and so allows penetration into the right brain.

Before beginning the induction routine, something must be said about the use of the word 'sleep'. As pointed out, hypnosis is the Greek for sleep. However, when you go to sleep you lose consciousness. In hypnosis this does not happen. So why do hypnotists frequently use phrases like 'You are now going to sleep'? We pointed out earlier that, in hypnosis, the aim is to link words with emotions or situations. The word 'sleep' is associated with two features of great importance: first, with closing your eyes; second, with the feeling of relaxation and 'letting go'. This 'letting go' is no more than 'shutting off' your left brain. It is, therefore, a very useful word. But at no time does a hypnotist mean fall into a 'natural' sleep. Unfortunately, some people do. Hypnotists are divided on the use of this word. Some replace it by the word 'trance'. I would suggest in the first instance you use 'sleep' in the knowledge that you are not expected to fall into a 'natural' sleep.

We are now in a position to go through an induction routine in detail. In this routine, the numbers refer to comments which will follow. The routine is specifically designed for someone hypnotizing themselves, and is an adaptation of a standard heterohypnotic induction routine. First, go to the toilet. Then seat yourself in a chair or lie down on a couch in as comfortable a position as you can. The light should be dim and external noise as low as possible. Now fix your eyes on some point – it really does not matter what it is. If you are sitting down, ideally it should be a little above your line of vision. Whatever happens, stare at the spot until your eyes close. Now, what follows, you should say mentally to yourself:

### Induction 1. Progressive Relaxation

My eyelids are becoming very, very heavy. Heavier and heavier; yes, my eyelids are becoming ever so heavy and they want to close. (1) With every breath I take, my eyelids are becoming heavier and heavier (pause). I am becoming very limp and relaxed, and as I become more limp and relaxed, so my eyelids are becoming heavier and heavier. With every breath I take, my eyelids are becoming heavier and heavier and they just want to close. (2) And all I want to do is relax and sleep (3) I am becoming more and more relaxed and all I want to do is sleep and relax; all I want to do is to fall into a very deep sleep, a very deep relaxed sleep (pause).

[Keep repeating until your eyes close. If they close sooner, just go straight on to the remaining instructions.]

My feet are very relaxed; my left foot is very relaxed. My left ankle is relaxed and as my left foot relaxes, so I am going into a deeper and deeper sleep. And now my left calf muscle is becoming very relaxed, very relaxed indeed (4). And the relaxation is spreading up my left leg into my left thigh. And now the whole of my left leg is becoming very relaxed and, as I relax more and more, so I am going into a deeper and deeper sleep. Not a natural sleep, but into a deep hypnotic sleep.

[Now do the same with the right leg.]

And now the relaxation is spreading up my body. My pelvis is very relaxed and, as I relax more and more, so I am going into a deeper and deeper sleep (pause). The muscles of my stomach are now relaxing. I am feeling very warm and comfortable and relaxed, and the more I relax so the deeper asleep I will go (pause). And now my chest muscles are relaxing, very, very relaxed. All my body is very relaxed, and, as I relax more and more, so I am going down and down into a deeper and deeper sleep, into a very relaxed deep sleep (pause).

My shoulder muscles are relaxing now. Very, very relaxed, just as all the other muscles have relaxed and are going to continue to relax. And so my shoulder muscles are relaxing and I am going down still deeper, yes down and down into a much deeper sleep (pause).

And now the muscles of my left arm are relaxing. They are becoming very limp and relaxed. All the muscles in my left arm are becoming very limp and relaxed. And now my left hand is also becoming very relaxed, just like the remainder of my body. And as I relax still further, so I am going into a much deeper sleep, not a natural sleep but a hypnotic sleep (pause). [Do the same for the right arm and right hand.]

Now the muscles of my neck are relaxing. Yes, they are becoming very relaxed indeed. All tension is going from my neck and the muscles are becoming very limp and relaxed (5). And, as the muscles of my neck relax, so I am sinking down into an even deeper and deeper sleep. The muscles of the back of my neck are becoming very relaxed indeed (6). And, as I relax, so I am sinking down into an ever deeper sleep.

And now the muscles of my face, my ears and around my eyes are relaxing. The muscles of my brow are relaxing. Yes, all the muscles of my face and head are becoming very relaxed, just like the rest of my body (7). And I am sinking into an ever deeper sleep (pause) (8).

[If you do not feel entirely relaxed by this stage, either concentrate on those parts where you believe tension still exists, or repeat the whole process from feet to head.]

Let us now take up the eight points. (1) If your eyes should begin to blink, don't worry. The best procedure if this happens is to incorporate it into the induction process – such as, 'As I blink, so I am becoming more and more relaxed and my eyelids will become heavier still, heavier and heavier with every blink'. (2) If the eyes close earlier, simply go on to the instructions referring to the feet. (3) We have mentioned already the use of the word 'sleep'. It is a convenient word because you associate with it the act of closing your eyes and with relaxing the body. Natural sleep is not intended, and this is repeated in the suggestions to emphasize the fact. (4) As you move up the body, something particular happens. As your attention switches from your feet to your calf muscles, then the feet will almost certainly relax more; and so on up your body. (5) At this stage, your head may fall to one side or forwards, if it has not already done so. This is especially true if you are sitting in a chair. Don't worry, just let it happen. If, however, this causes strain in the neck muscles, then put your head upright again – although it will repeatedly fall to one side. If this becomes troublesome, then this is a good sign to undertake

the session in a lying position. (6) The muscles of the back of
the neck are very important and the more they can be relaxed
by suggestion, the more relaxed you will feel overall. (7) By
now you should feel the muscles of your face relax. Your
mouth may open as your jaw relaxes. Again, just let things
happen. Pay no attention to them. (8) At the termination of all
this relaxation, you want somewhere to 'rest your mind'. Place
your attention at the centre of your forehead, between your
eyes – the location of the third eye. You will find that the mind
is quite happy to remain there without any effort on your part.

At this point you should be feeling very relaxed, your
thoughts somewhat sluggish and your breathing very low and
steady. You are, in fact, in a light hypnotic trance – some may
be much deeper. You should find this relaxed state very
pleasant indeed. It should be noted how the induction
routine, taken in its entirety, is directing the attention of the
mind to internal body sensations. Sensations, like emotions,
are features of the right brain and so the procedure 'closes
down' parts of the left brain and 'awakens' part of the right
brain. As the left brain 'shuts down', the mind focuses more
and more on the only stimulation it is receiving – namely, the
suggestions, in the form of words, a left brain activity. These
suggestions more readily pass into the right brain and so
generate a feeling or emotion of warmth and relaxation.

The length of time it takes to enter this light state of hypnosis
partly depends on how detailed your suggestions are and
partly on how adept you are at carrying out the instructions.
With practice, it becomes easier and quicker. In time, the
induction routine can be dropped altogether and a hypnotic
state achieved in a few minutes. But this comes later, after
practice of these preliminary exercises. You must walk before
you can run, as the saying goes.

### Termination of the Hypnotic State
Termination is remarkably easy, and amounts to no more
than suggesting that you will awaken with a specified word,
phrase or action. Here is a simple one you can use.

#### Termination Instruction
I am now going to count down from ten to one, I am now going

to count down from ten to one, and with each number I count, my sleep will become lighter and lighter, and when I reach the number 1, I shall be wide awake, yes when I reach the number 1, I shall be wide awake. And when I awaken I shall feel very relaxed, very fresh and very alert. Yes, when I awaken I shall feel very relaxed, very fresh and very alert. Ten, nine, lighter and lighter, eight, lighter still ... very light, one. Awaken.

As we have mentioned before, some people awaken with a slight headache, arising from the deep concentration. However, the suggestion to awake feeling relaxed, fresh and alert should prevent this. If you do have such a headache even after this suggestion, then simply suggest to yourself that when you awaken you will not have any headache, that you will be relaxed, fresh and alert and feeling much better for having relaxed and rested.

Another occurrence worth mentioning is that of awakening spontaneously for no apparent reason. This has probably something to do with the mood you are in, but why it occurs is not known. It is in no way harmful. This is to be contrasted from awakening spontaneously from an unpleasant sensation, or even a very extreme emotion. In this case, it is advisable to quickly re-hypnotize yourself and suggest calm and peace of mind, and then terminate the session as instructed above. The reason for doing it quickly, is simply because, at that stage, you are still very suggestible and hypnosis can be re-established fairly quickly. If you cannot re-hypnotize yourself, then the unpleasant feelings will wear off, just like any unpleasant feeling. But try again later. Short sessions can be most beneficial in establishing a quick response mechanism to the stimulus, i.e. the suggestions. These can be positively established by means of a post-hypnotic suggestion which will be outlined in Chapter 3.

If you do not awaken, this is probably because you are enjoying the hypnotic state; however, it could be because you have not cancelled a particular suggestion which may influence your behaviour in the waking state. If it is the former, then simply repeat the termination instructions. But this will be very rare in self-hypnosis because you would not have begun the termination instructions had you not wished to awaken in the first place! In the second case, always remember the basic rule: *always cancel any suggestion you have given yourself that you do not want to affect you in your waking state.* Suggestions that you do want to have an effect in your waking state are dealt with in Part II of this book.

## Other Induction Procedures
People vary in their response to the method of induction. The art is to find one that you are happy with. Generally, the simple induction method, given above, will work after a few attempts. If not, however, then it would be useful to know if some alternatives are available. I shall list a few here. The aim in each case is to reach the point of eye closure and relaxation. The simplest method, therefore, is to begin with your eyes closed and begin immediately with the body relaxation suggestions starting with your feet. The reason why some people may prefer this approach is because it avoids the challenge and 'prove it to me' attitude implied in eye closure. This also has the advantage of cutting down outside stimuli very early on in the procedure.

A quite different approach, suitable for self-hypnosis is the following. Take a coin and clasp it in your hand fairly tightly. Now stretch out your arm holding up your thumb and stare at the thumb nail. As you stare at the nail, repeat to yourself the following:

### Induction 2   Using a Coin
I am now relaxing and, as I relax, my fingers are becoming looser and looser. And the more loose they become, the more relaxed I am becoming. And when the coin drops, that will be the signal for me to close my eyes and fall into a very deep relaxed sleep, not a natural sleep but a hypnotic sleep. (pause) And now my grip is becoming lighter and lighter and I am relaxing more and more, and soon, very soon, I shall drop the coin. And when I drop the coin I shall also drop my arm, and when I do that I will close my eyes and fall into a pleasant deep sleep. Yes, I am becoming more relaxed and my fingers are becoming more and more loose.
[Keep repeating until the coin drops and you close your eyes. Then begin the relaxation suggestions given in Induction 1, beginning with your feet.]

A popular technique used by stage hypnotists is the 'hand clasp'. This can be very effective. To adapt it for self-hypnosis, try the following. First close your eyes and clasp your hands together in the normal way. Now begin the following series of suggestions:

### Induction 3  Using Clasped Hands

My hands are clasping tighter and tighter, and as they clasp tighter and tighter so I am becoming more and more relaxed and going into a deeper and deeper sleep. (pause)
Yes, I am going into a deeper and deeper sleep, the tighter my hands clasp together, and they *are* becoming tighter and tighter and I *am* becoming more and more relaxed, and going into a deeper and deeper sleep. (pause)
[Keep this up until you feel you are responding. When this happens, continue in the following manner.]
I am now relaxing my grip and as I relax my grip, so I shall go into an even deeper sleep, not a natural sleep, but a hypnotic sleep. And so as I relax my grip, as I *am* doing now, I am going even deeper asleep.
[Once your grip is loosened and you are relaxed, begin the relaxation suggestions given in Induction 1, beginning with your feet.]

The actual method of induction is not important, what *is* important is that you respond to it. The objective, in all cases, is to close off sensations from the outside world and re-direct your attention to your body sensations, whether it be to the heaviness in your eyelids, the thumb nail or your hands – they all serve the same purpose.

## Some Pointers in Giving Suggestions

Suggestions should be simple and direct, in fact the simpler, the better. They should be repeated frequently and, if possible, joined, so that a rhythm is maintained – which can be accomplished by the frequent use of the conjunctive 'and'. The most important is repetition. Repeat something often enough and you will respond because the suggestion will eventually register in the right brain. The repetition does not have to be exactly the same words, but close phraseology will have the greatest impact. A reconsideration of the suggestions given earlier will demonstrate the point of repetition.

It is worth commenting on why this works. When something is done or said for the first time, the left brain picks it up and processes it. More importantly, the left brain, (the seat of the conscious mind) carries out a reality-testing on such 'new' information. But if it is repeated, the reality-testing becomes unnecessary and, when this occurs, we relegate the stimulus to the right brain (i.e. to the unconscious mind) – we, in effect, don't hear it any longer.

We have all experienced this before: The clock in the room which guests hear but you do not; The house by the railway track or airport where the sound of the passing train or 'plane is not heard, etc. The brain has a natural mechanism for ignoring repetitive sounds once they become familiar, i.e. it passes the function to the right brain. You still 'hear', but now what matters is any change in the repetition. Thus, if the clock stopped you would immediately notice (consciously experience) the silence. The right brain has registered the change and passes a message back to the left brain. This process is more common than people realize. It occurs when you know that something is wrong or different, but cannot put it into words. The right brain is registering a change, but the left brain has not yet become sufficiently involved to put the feeling into words. The important point is that, once the suggestions are being picked up almost wholly by the right brain, no reality-testing takes place. Therefore, you eventually respond to the suggestions being made.

Another consideration is not to try too hard. Most people have, at one time or another, experienced the difficulty of getting to sleep at night, and the harder they try, the more difficult it becomes. They are suffering from what psychologists call the *principle of reverse effect*. Consider for a moment what people do to overcome the problem of not being able to get to sleep. Besides the counting of sheep, a more usual response is to pick up a book and read for a while, or go and make a night-cap. What this does is to direct the person's attention away from sleep and so breaks the circle of reverse effect. Soon the person becomes tired and eventually sleep comes.

Consider next a situation when you have forgotten a name.

The harder you try to remember it, the more distant the name appears. A first procedure is to run through the alphabet. Here you are hoping to make a correspondence between the letter and the person's name. Alternatively, you simply say: 'Let's pass over it, the name will come to me later' – and it often does *when you are least (consciously) thinking about it.* What has happened is that the right brain has continued the search and passes it across to your left brain, your conscious mind, like some revelation. Once again, the turning of attention to something else breaks the chain of reverse effect.

The same problem can happen in hypnosis. You may try too hard, and so set up a cycle of reverse effect, with the result that nothing happens. If this is the case, you must break the chain. Either stop and return to it at a later time, or stop trying so hard and just let things happen. In fact, letting things happen is the secret. Not forcing it to happen, but simply letting it happen. Thus, in the case of suggesting that the eyelids are becoming heavy, if you try too hard, they may never close. You must take a detached attitude and simply let what will happen, happen. Although this is easier said than done, it is important that you are able to recognize when you *are* trying too hard and *are* suffering from reverse effect. At least, if you recognize it, you can attempt to do something about it.

Associating suggestions is always a good idea. As the mind begins to turn towards bodily sensations, these can be coupled with suggestions to enhance the effect. For instance: 'As I become more and more relaxed, so I will become deeper and deeper asleep.' Here, we are coupling relaxation and sleep. Even a strong sensation can be coupled with relaxation. In the third induction procedure, based on the hand clasp, we had more than one coupling. As the hand clasp became tighter and tighter, so you were to become more and more relaxed *and* sleepier and sleepier. Each of these reinforces the other. The advantage of this particular coupling is that the harder you clasp your hands, the more this can be felt and hence, the more one believes the suggestions are working. The feeling of success makes further suggestions even more effective.

Another useful association is breathing and a particular suggestion – especially breathing and relaxation. There is a physiological reason for this. When you breathe out, your body naturally relaxes, (with deep breaths the feeling of relaxation when you breathe out is more noticeable). So if you suggest that, 'every time I breathe out I shall become more and more relaxed', then you will almost certainly do so. We shall see later in the book how we associate other bodily sensations with particular suggestions.

In the instructions, it should be observed that we have interposed 'pauses' fairly frequently. These are most important. As the mind slows down, so it requires time to absorb suggestions properly. Absorption is carried out during these pauses when little, if anything, should be thought. Such pauses are often overlooked, but psychological research shows that we read when our eyes pause, we learn best when it is done in units with pauses (breaks) at intervals. This is almost certainly because man, as an organism, operates according to cycles. We must be aware of these cycles and use them to our best advantage. Some pauses in the hypnotic sessions can be up to five minutes, but generally should not be longer.

## How do I Know that I am Hypnotized?
This is one of those questions like: 'How do I know whether I am in love?' All we can do is list features of the state. What is important is to recognize that hypnosis is a subjective experience, and you yourself will soon recognize the difference of the hypnotic state from other states of consciousness. This is not an unreasonable reply. Try to answer the question: 'How do you know you are awake?'

The main reason why some people find it difficult to know that they are hypnotized is simply because they are aware of everything, often *very* aware, when they expected something else. They are conscious and can hear and think in much the same way as normal. Those who are most surprised are the people who expect to become unconscious when they enter hypnosis. But, if you become unconscious, you could not give yourself instructions!, and if the difference in the states of consciousness is not so dramatic, the question remains unanswered.

Basically, at this stage, you will only have some indicators. First, you will feel very relaxed and peaceful. The muscles will be somewhat flaccid and you may feel your feet expand slightly. Also you may feel a tingling sensation throughout parts of your body – almost as if you can feel an exchange of energy taking place, (which is close to what in fact is happening). Your mind will feel sluggish and you may have difficulty remembering what you want to say. Don't worry, this is exactly what you want because it indicates that parts of the left brain are 'closing down'. Just carry on as if nothing had happened. Above all, *do not analyse what is happening*, for this will re-activate your left brain, your reasoning conscious mind, and this is the very thing you are attempting to suppress.

If your mind is at rest, along with your body, then you could very well be in a state where all you want to do is remain like that and not bother about anything. There is no danger of you remaining like this for long periods. Again, this is a state which you are trying to achieve. When this happens suggestions are carried out more readily because you neither want to resist, since this requires analysis, nor do you want to give the matter any thought, because this disturbs the tranquility that you are in. You simply want to experience the state. Thinking about this *now,* and not when it happens, the mind is taking the route of least resistance. This is sensible, because resistance requires an expenditure of mental energy, and this is wasteful. You expend most mental energy when you are anxious and worried, which is an unpleasant (and at times harmful) experience.

A more obvious sensation is the reduction in the heart rate as you relax, and, more particularly, a slow rhythmic breathing. Your breathing may become hardly perceptible. This is a useful indicator because it shows that the body is finding its own natural rhythm – a right brain function. The pace of life makes breathing and heart beat lose their natural rhythm, and more especially their *synchronization*. This is an important physiological change which is worth understanding. To illustrate the point, consider the following experiment – which, if you have a metronome, is worth trying.

Take a metronome and put it either on sixty beats to the minute or seventy-two beats to the minute. The first is the beat of largo music while the second is the usual pace of the heart beat. Now just sit quietly with your eyes closed. What you will find is that your own breathing and heart beat will slow down. More to the point, they will synchronize with the beat of the metronome. This should not surprise you. It is the principle behind lulling a baby to sleep, and relaxing by listening to slow orchestral music – especially baroque, which is usually at a tempo of sixty beats to the minute. The opposite also applies: In a car, if the music is lively, you tend to increase your speed, along with your heart beat.

You will find that this relaxation and synchronizing of heart beat and breathing is extremely beneficial. But relaxation will be discussed in further detail in Part II.

The most important thing to avoid at this, or any other stage, is the 'prove it to me' attitude. Simply accept things. The deepening suggestions supplied in the next chapter will give sufficient subjective experiences from which to sense that you are, indeed, in a hypnotic state.

# 3

# DEEPENING THE HYPNOTIC STATE AND POST-HYPNOTIC SUGGESTIONS

So far, we have considered how to induce a hypnotic state and how to terminate one. The time has now come to discuss how to deepen the state. Deepening techniques serve three purposes. First, they progressively take you, *in stages*, to deeper states and so increase your chance of success at whatever you intend to use the state to achieve. Second, it gives you a chance to become acquainted with your subjective feelings, and thus, to come to some understanding of what 'being hypnotized' actually means. This is more true in the case of the self-hypnotist, who obviously likes to think and feel that something is actually happening. Third, deepening techniques are used to assess the depth of hypnosis a person has reached. For the self-hypnotist, this third aspect is less important, what matters is that you learn to go as deep as possible – although even this is not essential for some uses to which hypnosis can be put.

Deepening is very much a question of finding out what you respond to best. Therefore, we shall list some of these, but once you have become proficient, then you can experiment, both with the deepening techniques given here, and others you may devise for yourself. Personal ones are always likely to be the most effective because these will be techniques that stimulate *your* right brain the most.

After the deepening techniques, I shall then discuss dissociation. This will consist of some introductory remarks about this subject because it is dealt with in detail in Chapter 7. Here, we shall concentrate on the use of dissociation as a means of deepening the hypnotic state.

In a later section, post-hypnotic suggestions will be dealt with. After discussing the nature of a post-hypnotic suggestion, I shall then deal with how it can be used to speed up the induction process, and to reach greater depth, quicker and easier on future occasions. In Part II of this book, a number of further uses of post-hypnotic suggestions will be examined.

The final section will deal with the use of additional aids, most specifically the use of cassette tapes. Making up your own tapes can be very useful, most especially for the person who is learning to hypnotize himself with no help from others whatsoever.

This will bring you to a point of knowing the basics of hypnosis: induction, deepening and termination. The remaining two chapters in Part I give more information about body sensations, (Chapter 4), and the use of visual imagery, (Chapter 5).

## Methods of Deepening

Counting downwards is a very popular technique for deepening, and is usually very effective. The idea is to use the numbers as signals to go deeper, and to intersperse the numbers with more suggestions of relaxation, etc. One point is worth mentioning, at this stage, which refers to other suggestions besides counting. Suggestions which involve you going *down* will tend to deepen the hypnotic state. For example, counting backwards, going down a lift, passing down a tunnel, etc. On the other hand, suggestions involving you going *up* tend to lighten the hypnotic state – although not necessarily. For example, counting upwards, climbing up a set of stairs, etc. This is by no means automatic, but it is worth bearing in mind when you are formulating your own suggestions. Here, then, is a simple instruction for deepening which involves counting downwards:

### Deepening 1   Counting

As I count down from ten to one, so I shall become more and more relaxed with each number I count, and I shall go deeper and deeper asleep with each number that I count. Deeper than before, and more deeply, easier than before with each number that I count (pause).

Ten. I am going deeper and deeper asleep, becoming more and more relaxed. Nine, yes I am finding it easier and quicker to go deeper and deeper asleep. Eight ...

Two. Deeper, much, much deeper asleep. Very relaxed and into a very pleasant relaxed deep sleep. One. I am now completely relaxed and very deeply asleep.

This particular technique can be very effective, especially if you respond to numbers. It is not essential to begin with ten. A higher number, such as one hundred, may be preferable because then you can continue counting down until you feel that you are sufficiently deep. If this technique *is* effective, then it can be made yet more effective by following the above instructions with another countdown, this time from one hundred, but in units of ten. The value of doing this is that you can first suggest that you will respond *as if* you had counted every number in between. You accordingly draw on your previous subjective experience and multiply it, as it were. Don't stop there. Count down from one thousand in units of one hundred. The beginning of the instructions can go something like this:

### Deepening 1 (continued)

I am now going to count down from one hundred in units of ten. With each number that I count, I shall go deeper and deeper asleep. I shall go deeper and deeper asleep, just as if I were responding to all the numbers in between, because with each number I will go into a much deeper sleep (pause).

One hundred, deeper and deeper. Ninety, I am going much, much deeper asleep. Very relaxed and sinking quickly and easily into a deeper sleep. Eighty, ...

The only unfortunate feature of this method, at least when it does not work, is that it is purely abstract and calls on no visualization – although you may find some form of imagery does come to mind. An alternative technique, therefore, is to combine the feature of counting down with some visualization, such as going down an escalator or down a lift. If you are afraid of either of these, then do not employ them in your visualization. This aside, you can visualize yourself, in your mind's eye, on the top floor and watch as you descend to the ground floor. If you know a shop or office block that you can readily call to mind, then do so. The technique is exactly like that of counting, except that you should, throughout, hold the picture in your mind's eye.

Deepening 2   Use of an Escalator
I am now going to go down the escalator. I am now on the fifth floor [or whatever], and as I go down on the escalator, so I will go down into a deeper and deeper sleep, and, as I reach each new floor, I will go extremely deep asleep (pause).
I am now stepping onto the escalator and going down, and down. I now step off onto the fourth floor and step, once again, onto the escalator. And as I go down, so I am going into a deeper and deeper sleep ...
I now step off on the ground floor and am very deeply asleep.

This technique of visualizing an escalator can be generalized to anything that appeals to you. If you know, for example, a garden with stairs going down to a pond or lake, then use this – or a pathway down a mountainside to the sea. Anything from your past experience that you can readily recall to mind. In all cases, go at a leisurly pace so that the suggestions have time to sink in. The more imaginative you are, the more responsive you will be to the suggestions to go deeper. We shall discuss the use of the imagination in Chapter 5.

The escalator or garden path use inner visual perception, i.e. picturing in the mind's eye, to aid in the deepening process. As we pointed out in Chapter 1, this is a function of the right brain. However, some people have this feature so under-developed that they cannot formulate pictures in their mind's eye. What, then, can be done? Such an individual requires a totally different technique that calls on a different right brain facility. The easiest sensation to elicit is heaviness, because when the body relaxes it tends to exhibit heaviness quite naturally – an unconscious person, for example, always appears heavier. This particular routine is best carried out sitting in a chair which has arms – although this is not essential. Have your arms resting on the arms of the chair and begin the suggestions as follows:

### Deepening 3   Heaviness in the Arms

My arms are becoming very, very heavy and, as they become very heavy, so I am sinking down into a deeper and deeper sleep. Yes, my arms are now becoming heavier and heavier, as heavy as lead, yes heavier than they have ever been before. And the heavier they become, the deeper asleep I will become, ... [Keep up the suggestions until you get a positive response.] And now my arms are becoming relaxed once again, all the heaviness is now going out of my arms and they are returning to the relaxed state they were in before.

This particular deepening technique has the advantage that you can feel something happening and that you are therefore responding to the suggestions. This is reassuring and so you will find that further suggestions are more readily carried out, because your belief in the power of suggestion has been verified.

Even individuals who respond very well to the deepening based on counting, should also attempt this deepening exercise. The exercise should be likened to the pianist practising his scales. The creation of heaviness, in itself, is not useful. But it is the easiest sensation that can be obtained by the use of suggestion. Once you have experienced this, you can progress to other, more involved, sensations and so, eventually, to those which are useful. You do not learn hypnosis instantaneously, it takes time and practice. The less developed your right brain, the more practice you need and the longer it takes. Most of the deepening instructions should be considered in this way; as exercises that will allow you to activate and experience sensations and emotions which take place, by suggestion alone, in the right brain.

An alternative to arm heaviness is the opposite, normally called arm levitation. The objective of this technique is to get your arm to feel very light and, the lighter it becomes, the deeper asleep you will become. This technique has the advantage that you can dictate the speed of your response. Furthermore, having the arm raised so that you touch your face has the advantage that the suggestion has its own built-in termination point, which can be used to enhance the deepening, most effectively. In the instruction to follow, no visual imagery is used. However, some people find that nothing happens. In this case, or in any case, employ some form of visualization. For instance, imagine your arm has a big balloon tied to it and the balloon begins to rise pulling your arm with it; or imagine that your arm is filled with helium gas – anything that has the implication (the response) of your arm rising. In these instructions, I shall refer to the right arm – either will do.

### Deepening 4   Lightness in the Arm

In a moment, I will find my right arm becoming lighter and lighter, and as it becomes lighter and lighter, so it will begin to rise. And as it rises, so I shall go into a deeper and deeper sleep. The deeper my sleep becomes, the lighter my arm will become and it will rise up higher and higher until I touch my right cheek with my hand, and when I touch my cheek with my right hand, that will be the signal to relax utterly and completely and the signal for me to sink into an extremely deep sleep indeed (pause). (Repeat if necessary.)

Now my right arm is becoming lighter and lighter, much, much lighter. And the lighter it becomes so the deeper my sleep is becoming.

[When your arm touches your cheek and you feel a greater surge of relaxation and deepening, just let it happen, let the feeling take hold and give yourself no further suggestions for some minutes.]

The next technique, lid catalepsy, can, at its best, be very effective or, at its worst, simply terminate the session. It is the most effective of the deepening techniques which demonstrates that you are in a hypnotic state, and so it is worth finding out whether you respond to it. Luckily, most people do. If you do not, however, you can always return to it when you are better at creating the hypnotic state. It is a very simple technique, almost too simple. Its success arises from making the suggestions repetitive enough – and with visual imagery if possible.

The object is to suggest that the eyelids are very heavy, so heavy that you cannot possibly open them, and that the more you try to open them, the heavier they will become. When successful, you will know it, and this reinforces the knowledge, (and confidence) that you are hypnotized. This makes further suggestions more readily accepted. The negative aspect is if you *do* open your eyes. The conclusion generally drawn from this is that you are not hypnotized (even though you are likely to be in a light trance). The lack of success makes further suggestions less likely to be successful. For the self-hypnotist the message is simple. Try it a few times. If it works, use it; if it doesn't work, try one of the others, but return to this technique when you are more proficient. *All* techniques can be accomplished eventually. The suggestion goes like this:

### Deepening 5  Sticking of the Eyelids

My eyelids are becoming very heavy, so heavy that I cannot open them. The harder I try to open them, the heavier they will become and it will be impossible to open them. My eyelids are so very, very heavy that I cannot open them. The more I try to open them, the heavier they will become, they will be so very, very heavy that I will not be able to open them. They will be so heavy that it will feel as if my eyelids are stuck together, stuck tightly together, so tightly that I cannot possibly open them. [Repeat if necessary. Now try to open them – *not* while repeating the above suggestions. After some attempt, and getting a feel for the reaction to the suggestions, continue as follows.]

Now, relax, relax the eyelids, just relax. I am now relaxed and I can open my eyes at any time I wish. At the moment I don't want to, but I can open them from now on, if I want to, with no difficulty at all.

It is very important to cancel the suggestion, as shown here. This cancelling of suggestions should become habitual, cancelling all those suggestions that you do not want to linger into the waking state.

Another deepening technique which uses body sensations is limb rigidity. We shall not give the instructions in great detail because they are just like those given for the eyes. In this case, you simply state that your arm (right or left) is becoming stiff, straight and rigid – like a statue, a pencil, or whatever comes to mind that is stiff, straight and rigid. Also, it is useful to add that the more stiff and rigid your arm becomes, the deeper asleep you will go. This is a very useful technique because you can sense the tension and stiffness occurring in your arm, which reassures the success of the suggestions. On completion, suggest that your arm, once again, is to relax. You will probably find that the relaxation occurs much quicker than the stiffness, especially on the first few occasions.

Of course, stiffness can be suggested in the legs or even the whole body, and some variety can be used on different occasions. This particular suggestion, like the others, is not useful in itself, but it does have the advantage that it gives you a clearer sense about muscle tensions and the difference between a tense muscle and a relaxed one. This is a point which will be developed in Chapter 6, when I shall discuss relaxation in detail.

One final technique, which can also be most effective, is that of rolling your arms around one another. You simply start this rolling motion at a steady slow pace and then begin your suggestions:

### Deepening 6  Rolling the Arms

My arms are going to go around faster and faster, faster and faster, and the faster they go, the deeper asleep I shall go. They are now going faster still, faster still, and the faster they go the deeper asleep I will go.
[Keep repeating until the response is clearly established.]

Again, the response is very obvious and so reinforces the suggestion. Furthermore, this technique has its own natural rhythm which creates a feedback mechanism.

All the deepening techniques given here do not need to be applied on the same occasion. If you wish to become proficient at self-hypnosis, however, they should all be tried at one time or another – as well as any others you may come across or invent. By noting which you respond to the best, you gain some information about your right brain. For instance, some people respond well to counting, but are poor at visualizing pictures; others find that they respond best when suggestions are coupled with motor responses, such as that of arm rolling.

There is little doubt that the more such suggestions can be coupled with visual imagery, the more effective they will be. As shall be outlined in detail in Chapter 5, the more vivid, and even the more bizarre, the imagery, the better. This should be no surprise. When you dream, the more vivid the dream, the more emotional content there is associated with it. What is happening when you use imagery is that you are using features of the right brain more efficiently. An image created in the right brain will give rise to physical and physiological responses in the remainder of the body *that are consistent with the image being created*. Take the eyes being tightly closed in instruction 5. When you are telling yourself that you cannot open your eyes, imagine that they are glued together – see the glue being plastered on. Or imagine that there is a zip on your eyelids and the zip is pulled closed. As has been constantly pointed out, the more bizarre, the more the suggestions are likely to be effective.

### Dissociation: a First Discussion
The self-hypnotist has a major disadvantage in comparison with the heterohypnotic situation. In the latter case, the person being hypnotized can, if they are willing, sink into a very deep state because they can more fully shut down their left brain. But the self-hypnotist cannot accomplish this to the same degree, because he has still to formulate suggestions and take a very positive act in creating the necessary change in state – both of which are undertaken with the left brain. This means that the most successful at self-hypnosis are those individuals who can dissociate.

Dissociation is not something new to the individual; we have all used it on various occasions, but to differing degrees. The most obvious example of everyday dissociation is when a person remarks: 'Just stand back and look at the situation', or: 'Let's look at this objectively'. What they mean is that they need to detach themselves from the emotional involvement so that an objective viewpoint can be taken. Who is doing the act and who the observing? Another example, more closely associated with being in a hypnotic state, is when you perform something very mechanically, as if your body was doing the work, but your mind is elsewhere. To say that something is being done mechanically means that the function has been taken over by the right brain and so requires no conscious effort on your part. This leaves the left brain to occupy itself with something else – the shopping or whatever. During these dissociated states, you can even get the feeling of 'observing yourself' at the work in hand. A third example we have already remarked on, namely involvement in reading or watching a movie. Your mind and body seem to have temporarily parted company: become detached. All these are everyday examples of dissociation.

Dissociation is not the same as multiple personality, but they do have a number of features in common. It is possible to argue that multiple personality is not possible if a person cannot dissociate. More importantly, to increase the ability to dissociate does not mean that you will develop multiple personality. Multiple personality is a psychological disorder, while dissociation is an ability we all possess and all utilize on occasions. (The most famous cases of multiple personality are those of Eve – made famous in the film *The Three Faces of Eve* – and Sybil, who had no less than sixteen personalities! These make for fascinating reading and two accessible sources are given in the list of references.)

Given that we all dissociate, the art is to enhance this ability and to utilize it at the appropriate time. I have found one technique very useful in achieving this, and it has the advantage of being extremely simple. Studies by psychologists have demonstrated that we respond very much to our own name, most especially our personal (first) name or some nickname we particularly like. In my own case I use 'Ronald'. The idea is to suppose that 'I' is the person giving the instructions, and hence located in the left brain, while 'Ronald' is the person carrying out the instructions, and located very much in the right brain.

Deepening instructions now take the following form:

Ronald, you are going deeper and deeper, with every number that I count you are going deeper and deeper. Yes, Ronald, you are very responsive to my suggestions and, with each number I count you are going down into a much deeper sleep ...

There is more to it than simply separating 'I' from 'Ronald'. When combined with visual imagery, the 'I' can become the observer of 'Ronald'. Suppose, for instance, you have had a very hectic day and you are very tense. Suppose that the techniques given so far do not seem effective because your tensions are running too high. Then you could imagine that you, i.e. 'Ronald', is being massaged. The 'I' repeats the suggestions from some point outside the body and you imagine yourself, i.e. 'Ronald', being massaged. Notice that three 'persons' are involved. The one sitting in the chair, the one observing, and the one being massaged. Once you have the image as clear as possible in your mind's eye you can begin:

Ronald, you are relaxing all your muscles, very relaxed, and you are going into a deep relaxed sleep. As you are rubbed so you are becoming more and more relaxed, and as you relax so you will find it easier and easier to follow all my suggestions ...

It is important to have the picture as vivid as possible and actually *feel* the relaxation coming to the various parts of your body. The picture is aided by the fact that you are considering yourself observing the scene.

Another use of the personal name and 'I' as being separate is to assume that 'I' is a hypnotist and you, 'Ronald', are the subject. This can be very effective for someone who has some resistance to going deeper. In making it most effective, you must believe that the hypnotist is very proficient and you, the subject, are going to be extremely responsive to the suggestions. As you observe it, so it will be.

Dissociation is most helpful to the self-hypnotist because it allows you to take advantage of what is called 'trance logic'. This term simply refers to the fact that, in a hypnotic state, you can simultaneously perceive yourself doing one thing (being massaged, say), but at the same time know that you are sitting in the chair, and yet experience no sense of inconsistency.

A more extreme example may help. In Chapter 7 we shall discuss a situation of dissociation where you observe yourself stepping out of your body and 'looking' at yourself in the chair. Now suppose this has taken place. If asked what you are doing, a likely response is: 'Looking at myself in the chair'. If you were then asked: 'But then who is the person observing you in the chair?', the likely response is: 'That is also me'. To the hypnotized person, there is nothing 'illogical' about this, it appears internally consistent within 'trance logic'. What is demonstrated here is the right brain's facility to use symbols and synthesis to create a sensation or emotion – which it does each night in dreams. Once 'trance logic' is accepted by the hypnotized person, then any inner conflicts tend to be reduced and so a deeper hypnotic depth can be attained.

## Post-Hypnotic Suggestions

A post-hypnotic suggestion refers to a suggestion which is given to a person when in a hypnotic trance and which involves an action to be carried out later when the person is in the waking state. Take the following example, which is simple and of no particular use in itself, except to demonstrate typical, post-hypnotic behaviour. When in a hypnotic state, suppose you gave yourself a suggestion that when you awoke after five minutes you would have a tremendous desire to take off your right shoe, and that with each moment that passed this urge would become stronger and stronger until you took off your right shoe. If you were actually carrying this out you would use repetition and imagery. Now, in all probability, you will carry out this instruction. After five minutes has elapsed, you will find all your attention constantly being directed to your right shoe. You will remember this post-hypnotic suggestion, but still the urge to comply will get stronger and stronger until you carry it out.

If a post-hypnotic suggestion is not carried out, two reasons are usually advanced to explain this. First, the person was not in a sufficiently deep enough trance. Second, the instruction was ridiculous, inconsiderate or improper. Let me take each of these in turn. The first explanation is certainly true in a number of occasions, but it is a fallacy to conclude the depth of hypnosis from the fact of whether or not a given post-hypnotic suggestion is carried out. Post-hypnotic suggestions, if reasonable, can be acted upon with the person being in a light to a very deep trance.

The second explanation has arisen largely from experimentation and stage shows. If you are given a ridiculous instruction (in heterohypnosis or in self-hypnosis), then, in all likelihood, you will not comply. The same is true if the suggestion, in some way, went against your moral code. It appears that the super-ego, to use a Freudian concept, is always working and does not go to 'sleep'. The point here is that these situations tend to arise in heterohypnosis where a ridiculous suggestion is being used in experimental work to 'demonstrate' the existence of post-hypnotic phenomenon, or by stage hypnotists who wish to create an amusing performance (at the cost of the volunteer). In self-hypnosis, this is unlikely to arise because you are unlikely to give yourself ridiculous or improper post-hypnotic suggestions.

The great importance of post-hypnotic suggestions are their use in speeding up the induction process on future occasions and in creating useful and beneficial behaviour patterns. In the remainder of this section, I shall deal with its use in speeding up the induction routine on future occasions, leaving the second aspect to be dealt with in appropriate sections in Part II of this book.

For the person learning self-hypnosis, the use of post-hypnotic suggestion is most important. The basic idea is that when you have induced hypnosis you give yourself a suggestion to the effect that, on the next occasion and all future occasions, you will go into a hypnotic state immediately a particular cue or signal is given. You continue with the suggestion that you will respond immediately the signal is given, and that you will easily and quickly reach a very deep hypnotic state. In a moment I shall supply a useful, detailed post-hypnotic instruction for this purpose.

Your first task, however, is to choose some *simple* signal. This can be a word, a phrase or some action. It should be given some careful consideration because you will, in fact, use it repeatedly. More importantly, it should be something that is not commonly done. Suppose, for instance, that you chose as a signal the act of snapping your fingers. If you were successful in your post-hypnotic suggestion then each time you snapped your fingers you would close your eyes and go into a hypnotic state! The same is true if you chose a simple word like 'sleep'. If you wish to choose a single word it should be one you know well, but which you would not use in general conversation. For this reason a phrase is better – along the lines: 'When I say ... I shall immediately fall into a deep hypnotic state', where the dots refer to your chosen phrase which is going to act as a signal. If it is some action, the same considerations apply. It should be something you would not normally do.

One possibility is to *combine* a simple action with a simple phrase, and both must be done simultaneously to act as a signal. In this way the action can be an everyday action, like putting your hands together as in prayer, and the word can be simple, such as 'sleep'. Whatever signal you choose, the post-hypnotic suggestion should make it absolutely clear that you will respond only when you yourself give the signal. Although this may have been assumed, it is better to incorporate it into the suggestion, so that there is no doubt as to what is to be expected.

Before giving the instructions, one final point is worth making. A post-hypnotic suggestion can and does wear off. It is therefore important to repeat it very frequently. On future occasions, the instructions can be very brief, no more than reminding yourself of the signal (the stimulus), and what you should do when the signal is given (the response). For those familiar with Pavlov's experiments done with dogs, it is clear that the stimulus-response behaviour is being reinforced so that it becomes automatic. From what has been said so far in this book, it should be clear that, after sufficient repetition, the response behaviour is automatically done by the right brain, i.e. the signal has a direct route from the left brain and into the right brain. In this way, future inductions can take a few minutes, or even less. In this lies the importance of post-hypnotic suggestions – and not in performing ridiculous actions for amusement.

Now for the post-hypnotic instruction for inducing an immediate trance on all future occasions. In this we shall use a phrase, denoted ..., as the signal.

**Post-hypnotic Suggestion: Speeding Up Induction**
[Name], in the future, whenever you say to yourself... you will immediately close your eyes and fall into a deep hypnotic state. Yes, whenever you say to yourself ... you will immediately fall into a deep hypnotic state. Each time you say to yourself..., you will respond easier and quicker than the time before, you will fall into a deep hypnotic trance whenever you say this, quicker than on the previous occasion and you will go deeper than on the previous occasion.

Yes, [name], when you say ..., you will immediately fall into a deep hypnotic sleep. And if anyone else should say ..., then nothing will happen. It is only when you say to yourself..., that you will immediately fall into a deep hypnotic trance, easier than the time before and quicker than the time before.

And on each future occasion you will relax far more than ever before, and because when you relax you will go deeper asleep, then you will go much deeper asleep in the future.

And all this will happen whenever you say .... Because from now on, whenever you say to yourself ..., you are going to immediately close your eyes and sink quickly and easily into a very deep hypnotic state.

One procedure to make this more effective is to dissociate, and when in a dissociated state, let the 'I' be giving these instructions while you are sitting or lying listening to them. In this way, the instructions reach the right brain more effectively and so the post-hypnotic suggestion is likely to be more successful. Notice in this instruction, the constant use of the signal so that it clearly becomes embedded in your unconscious. Keep using this even when you are successful. Then, however, you can shorten the instruction considerably.

## Additional Aids
For the self-hypnotist the major difficulty is always shutting off parts of the left brain while still keeping enough conscious control to give suggestions. We pointed out in a previous section how dissociation can help in this regard. Another method is the use of cassette tapes. This is a half-way house between heterohypnosis and self-hypnosis. Once you can readily enter the hypnotic state, then it is possible to use tapes

with instructions for deepening, for post-hypnotic suggestions, or any other suggestions that you may want to give – some of which shall be discussed in Part II of this book. It is even possible to put the whole induction, deepening and termination routine on the one tape. This has the advantage that you can sit back and just let things happen. Taping the post-hypnotic suggestion, given in the previous section, is extremely useful for the self-hypnotist because a greater hypnotic depth can be achieved and so the greater the possibility of success.

The general routine is exactly the same as we have outlined, so far, in this book. But some comments on the use of cassette tapes is worthwhile. We shall discuss four aspects:

   (i)   The very beginning of the induction.
  (ii)   Deepening – involving a specified reaction in a specified time.
 (iii)   How to deal with an emergency when you are alone.
  (iv)   What if you don't wake up when the termination instruction is given?

If you tape an induction which begins with your eyes open, and it contains suggestions that your eyelids will become heavier and heavier, then this has the disadvantage that your eyes may close before the instruction to close them is given. This can be annoying. The way out of this is either to begin with your eyes closed and start the toe-to-head relaxation, or, alternatively, simply say to close your eyes when you count to three. Then continue to ten suggesting relaxation and sleep. Pause, and then begin the toe-to-head relaxation suggestions.

The same idea applies to deepening. Counting is useful because you simply respond to the suggestions. Arm heaviness is useful because if you do not respond fully then this will not hold back the next suggestion. This is why raising your arm may not be so useful on tape. If you do not respond by the time the tape thinks you have, it will finish the suggestion without any response on your part, which may act negatively on your unconscious mind. This also applies to arm rigidity. Eye catalepsy is useful if you respond to it without opening your eyes. If, however, you do open your eyes this suggestion should be removed from the tape – but first try the tape a few times.

If you do respond to the tape, it may be that you do not hear noises such as the noise of passing cars or the refrigerator. The worry may then arise that you will not hear the telephone ring, a knock at the door, or some emergency. This is not true. It is well known that a mother can sleep soundly and not awaken, even with fairly loud bangs, but will awaken immediately the slightest sound occurs from her baby. This facility of specific attention is by no means restricted to mothers or to the state of sleep. A well-documented situation is that of hearing your own name in a party bustling with noise. You may even be able to hear and respond to the person you are with, but be paying attention to another conversation about which you are particularly interested. Although you are withdrawing your senses from outside stimuli, you can always 'hear' them, but you do not generally register them in your consciousness.

When you tape a session, therefore, a fairly early suggestion should be one which involves reassurance that you will awaken immediately if the need arises. The suggestion can go something like this:

### Taping a Reassurance Instruction

You know that, even when you sleep at night, you have in you a safeguard to awaken you in an emergency, so during your hypnosis the same guard will awaken you if the door bell or telephone rings, or if an emergency occurs that requires your immediate attention. Yes, you will immediately awaken if something requires your immediate attention. And you will have no difficulty awakening. And so if the tape should get entangled or stop for some reason, then for this too you will immediately awaken.

And because you know that, for whatever reason, you will awaken if the need arises, then this will ease your mind and so allow you to give yourself up, utterly and totally to this hypnotic session, in the knowledge and confidence that you will immediately awaken if the need arises. Now relax, sleep and give yourself up to the hypnotic sleep.

Let us suppose the tape runs through its suggestions and comes to the last which terminates your hypnosis, but you do not wake up. In one respect this should not happen if you have responded to the suggestions prior to this one, but let us suppose you have, but still do not awaken because you do not consider this an 'emergency' and you are feeling pleasantly relaxed. Either you can simply repeat to yourself the termination suggestions, or if you are very deep you will come out naturally because the hypnotic depth cannot be maintained in periods of prolonged silence. You may even fall into a natural sleep from which you will also awaken as from a light nap. This is most unlikely, but we have discussed it here to allay any concern that you may have and to show how to deal with the unexpected if it should happen. Never worry, and simply continue the suggestions. If you are truly hypnotized (for how else could you not awaken!) then you respond to suggestion: hence, simply continue the suggestions and you are bound to respond very soon.

Two other aids are worth considering. One is the use of the metronome, while the other is the use of music. We shall take these in turn. The metronome we have already encountered. Its value lies in the monotonous sound at a regular rhythm. It can be used either during induction and/or as a means of deepening. In both cases it is best set at seventy-two beats a minute – the heart beat. If it is used during the induction then it can replace looking at some point. You can, however, continue to look at a point while listening to the metronome. Alternatively, you can fix your eye on the swing of the bar while listening to the click. Some people respond to this very quickly. If used during deepening, you can suggest to yourself that with every click you will go deeper and deeper asleep. There is one difficulty in using the metronome in deepening when you are on your own, and that is that it may have totally unwound, which limits its use. One way to overcome this problem is to tape the click of the metronome, say, taking up one whole side of a cassette tape. The tape can then be employed as background during the induction and also used for deepening.

The fact that the sound will be so regular means that the left brain will soon ignore its presence and pass it to the right brain. This will then influence your breathing and heart beat, so as to establish a synchronized pattern.

Just as the metronome can be used as background, so too can music – but not any kind of music. The first point is that the music must not be vocal and must either be a solo instrument or an orchestra. The music must be soft and slow. Films occasionally show Indians meditating with classical Indian music in the background. This is just what is needed. The Western music most suitable for this purpose is classical baroque, such as Handel. However, what matters is that it is slow and soothing. It does not have to be all the one composition and can be made up by putting together appropriate pieces from individual records – such as all largo music. It is important that you find the music pleasing. If it jars, then delete it from the tape. There may be an unconscious reason for this dislike. To illustrate the point, the music may remind you of the seashore with the waves lapping on the rocks. For many people this can conjure up a most pleasing and soothing sensation. If, however, you lost a loved one in such a place, then such music will only bring to mind hurtful memories. This is an extreme example, but when something jars, the unconscious mind is sending out a signal that you should not ignore.

Before leaving aids, it is possible to combine them if you have two tape decks. This can be most effective. On one cassette tape you can have all your suggestions and on another the click of the metronome or music. Simply play the two together – but not loudly. You may find that the music or the metronome reinforces the suggestions and makes them more effective. This is now the basis of some learning techniques being pursued, especially in Russia.

# 4
# CHARACTERISTICS OF THE HYPNOTIC STATE

In this chapter I wish to explore in more detail what happens during the induction and deepening procedures. In particular, I shall concentrate on the frame of mind being created, the bodily sensations likely to be experienced and some other points – such as the likelihood of falling into a natural sleep, the difficulty of holding thoughts, the sudden mental change that may be experienced, and the cyclic nature of hypnosis.

It is clear, from the list just given, that we shall be concerned very much with subjective experiences which, by their very nature, are particular to the person experiencing them. Two choices are open. Either nothing is said and the self-hypnotist finds out for himself; or, alternatively, some *common* experiences can at least be highlighted. The second approach seems preferable because there *are* common experiences which the majority of persons being hypnotized, whether by someone else or by oneself, will encounter. The precise form and intensity will, however, vary. Even so, a discussion of some of these will allay any additional worries the self-hypnotist may have. To be forewarned is to be forearmed.

## Feelings During Induction and Deepening
We have already pointed out that hypnosis, as a procedure,

reduces sensory information to the brain to an absolute minimum. In so doing, the brain, which never stops working, turns inwards to body sensations. These are normally present, but do not consciously enter awareness because they are 'drowned' by all the other sensory input – from sight, sounds, touch and smell. We have all had experience of this with respect to a pain. A pain seems to come and go in our conscious awareness. If something happens, or a film captures our interest which requires our attention, then the pain is temporarily not 'felt', but then, a short while later, our attention returns to the pain and the awareness of the pain returns. The point is that we are only consciously aware of the pain when we direct our attention towards it. How often does a mother exclaim: 'Don't think about it and the pain will go away!'? What these remarks illustrate is that our body sensations are generally not considered at the conscious level, because the brain is processing other information which occupies all of a person's conscious awareness. Only when we relax and shut off outside stimuli is our attention turned inwards to such bodily sensations.

The first sensation to be experienced, therefore, is a slowing down. This arises from the fact that there is very little for the mind to concentrate on, except the suggestions – which are slow, repetitive and melodious. During the early stages of the induction, other thoughts begin to cross the mind, such as whether you have fed the cat, almost as if the mind just abhors having nothing to think about. Soon these 'pressing' thoughts become less and less as the mind quietens down. In fact, one object of the induction *is* to reduce such extraneous thoughts as much as possible. One way to do this is to let them simply pass through the mind and, above all, pay them no attention. To consider that they are hindering your induction process is, in fact, to pay attention to them, and you can only do this by holding them in your consciousness. Pay them no attention and simply let them pass through your mind. The aim is to be purely passive. Soon your attention will rest wholly on your own suggestions.

The second sensation is that of relaxation and heaviness. This is the object of the induction and if it is working, then you should feel relaxed, and, as you relax, a feeling of heaviness should develop. The induction routine, outlined in Chapter 2, is especially designed to enhance these feelings. As you move up your body, the part *prior* to the one you are presently concentrating on, will relax even more. For instance, as you direct your attention away from your right leg to your left leg, the right leg will almost certainly relax even more than it already is. The principle of redirected attention is being utilized here. When you cannot get to sleep, the more you think about it, the more difficult it seems to become. We discussed this earlier, in terms of the principle of reverse effect. The point is that when your conscious thoughts are dealing with one thing, your unconscious can be dealing with the thing you really want. So when the conscious thoughts are attending to relaxing the left leg, the unconscious is relaxing even more the right leg. And so on up your body.

I shall deal fully with relaxation by means of hypnosis in Chapter 6, but it is important to realize that, as you become more relaxed and limp, so you will not wish to move any muscle in your body. It is this which you should aim at achieving. You will find it very pleasant. To move your body will feel as if it is too much trouble, and totally unnecessary at that. If achieved properly, then doing some of the deepening exercises which involve moving specific parts of the body will not disturb the overall relaxation which has been achieved. Furthermore, if, after each exercise, you suggest to yourself that you are once again relaxed, then this is what you will be – almost immediately.

Once relaxation is achieved, if not before, you may experience a tingling sensation, especially in the legs and feet. The feet may even feel as if they are slightly expanding. These reactions are quite normal and can give the feeling of vitality. This is almost certainly the case. At particular times, a person can either take in energy from the environment or can give up energy to the environment. When you relax you give your body an opportunity to draw this much-needed energy, and there is some tentative evidence that this is a feature of the right brain. When a person is ill or run-down they are asked to rest. Through rest and relaxation the body can restore its energy reserves. This tingling sensation is most conspicuous in the early stages of induction and seems to taper off as you establish some form of equilibrium.

A most characteristic experience of relaxation and further deepening is the slowing down of the heart beat and of the breathing. The breathing especially becomes very mild and takes on a slow steady rhythm, sometimes imperceptible. As you learn to relax, this feature is very soon established. It shows that the body is establishing its own natural rhythm, which it finds the best for relaxation and other body functions. It is very therapeutic and if you do not experience this change in breathing, it almost certainly means that you have not sufficiently relaxed.

One aspect of breathing is worth commenting on. When very relaxed, and breathing is slow and steady you may experience, on occasions, an expelling of air, as if there was an air pocket. Some authors have commented on the phenomenon, but have not given any reason for it. However, it seems to me that this is highly significant. There is a view in physiology that tension, that has not found any outlet, is retained by the body in the muscles. The obvious case is the person who 'bottles up his emotions' and has stomach cramp or a peptic ulcer. Tense or anxious people have tense expressions because their muscles are tense. It is even argued that such tension simply accumulates, unless dispelled in some way. Now during hypnosis, as the body truly relaxes, these tensions are released. It is very probable that when these deep-seated tensions in the muscles are released some physiological change takes place, which has, as one of its features, an expulsion of air. This is one of the reasons why relaxation is so therapeutic.

## The Likelihood of Entering Natural Sleep

It has probably crossed your mind that if you relax, as suggested, then you may fall into a natural sleep. This is possible, but rather unlikely. The hypnotic state, although often referred to as 'sleep', (the word used frequently in suggesions), is not like ordinary sleep at all. The word 'sleep' is useful because you already have an idea that sleep is associated with 'letting go' and relaxing. This is why the word is so frequently used by hypnotists. Some hypnotists, however, dispense with the word altogether and merely suggest limpness and relaxation. Hypnosis is an active state, to a large extent, requiring your co-operation and participation. Natural sleep does not involve this degree of co-operation and participation.

Having said this, what would happen if you became so relaxed that you did fall to sleep? Well, you would simply respond as you always do when you fall asleep. In your own time, or when disturbed, you would awaken. You will no longer be in a hypnotic state and you will awaken in the same state as when you awaken from a natural sleep.

A situation in which you are most likely to fall into a natural sleep when hypnotizing yourself, is if you have taken 'too much' alcohol or some soporific drug, e.g. hayfever tablets. The relaxation plus the drug is likely to lead very quickly into a loss of concentration and into a natural state of sleep. Hypnosis, both self-hypnosis and heterohypnosis, is best undertaken with a clear head and no other stimulants. In fact, one of the main values of hypnosis is to deal with the very situations that may be leading you to take alcohol or tablets. We shall not deal in this book with medical uses of hypnosis and anyone interested in these aspects will find W.S. Kroger and J. Hartland useful to consult.

## Difficulty in Holding Thoughts

The induction and deepening aims at reducing sensory inflow and at shutting down, to a large extent, the left brain, the conscious mind. As you become successful at this, what you may find is difficulty in remembering your own instructions or suggestions. It is as if the conscious mind 'blanks out' for short periods. Rather than being alarmed at this, it is a sign of success. Simply ignore it and carry on, or go back and repeat your suggestions.

In heterohypnosis, this is more likely to happen, but here you do not have to do a 'double act' and so you can give in to the state and lose all consciousness. The self-hypnotist must always preserve that small degree of consciousness in order to give himself instructions. If, however, you use recorded tapes, as outlined in the last chapter, you may find loss of consciousness occurs more frequently because then, as in heterohypnosis, you can let go more completely.

## Sudden Mental Change

As the induction and deepening takes hold, you will find that you will accept further suggestions more readily. You may even get the feeling that there is nothing you would not do. Occasionally, however, another change occurs which, unlike this gradual realization, is very sudden. With your concentration in the centre of your head between the eyebrows, on some occasions you will find a sudden change occurs in your mental outlook. The most obvious sensation is the absolute clarity of your thought processes. It is as if you have 'jumped' onto another plane of consciousness. When this happens, it is quite unmistakeable because, qualitatively, it is so different both from your thoughts when awake, and your thoughts during the early stages of induction and deepening. During this state, you are at your most responsive and so many important suggestions you wish to give yourself should be done when this occurs.

If you find that you have not achieved this, one possible reason is that you have not included any long periods of silence when no suggestions at all are made. The 'jump' is most likely to occur during one of these periods.

## Cyclic Nature of the Hypnotic State

The hypnotic state does not deepen gradually or continuously, nor does it necessarily level off at some lower limit, as drawn in Figure 4(a). It, in fact, cycles with a downward trend, as illustrated in Figure 4(b). This should come as no surprise. The body is an electro-chemical apparatus in large part, and even the mechanical aspects, like heart beat, behave in waves. This cyclic feature of hypnosis reveals the changing impulses in the brain. We now know, from research on altered states of consciousness, of the importance played by alpha waves, beta waves and theta waves. Of these three waves, the important one in hypnosis, as in meditation, is the alpha pattern. These occur as the mental processes are slowed down, as we have already talked about. The point being made here is that the hypnotic state varies in a wave pattern. You can recognize yourself, that during a hypnotic session you are sometimes very deep indeed, while at other times, during the same session, you may feel as if you are about to awaken. At the same time, the deepening trend is also quite apparent. A discussion of alpha waves and their occurrence in altered states of consciousness can be found in H. Bloomfield *et al.*, given in the references.

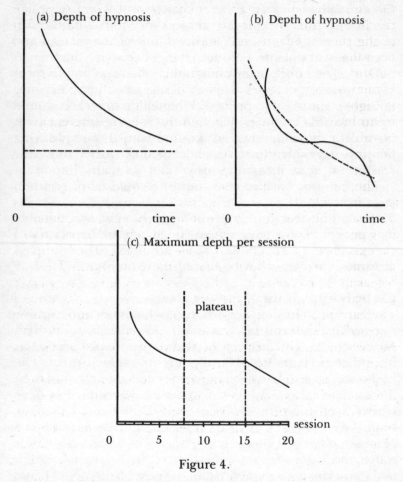

Figure 4.

Some authors argue that the depth that a person can reach is fairly fixed and cannot be exceeded – shown by the dotted line in Figure 4(a). This is not true, and is a negative attitude which must be avoided at all costs. This is not to say that in any particular session there is no lower limit, or that over some consecutive sessions only a certain depth can be reached. But these should be thought of as 'plateaux', as illustrated in Figure 4(c). We are familiar with plateaux in many learning situations, e.g. learning a sport, learning to type, or learning a hobby. Why should learning hypnosis be any different? It is my contention that there *are* plateaux and when these are reached a change in approach or more ingenuity is required in giving suggestions in order to break out of the plateau and onto the next phase.

One typical plateau encountered is when you have doubts about whether, in fact, you are going deeper. Such a negative thought is sure to hold up the deepening process. You should try to believe absolutely that continued deepening is always possible, that Samadhi is attainable, and that the only thing holding you back is knowing how to do it and finding the reason for the lack of progress.

The view that only a certain depth can be reached seems to arise from laboratory experiments on hypnosis. Valuable as these are, they very rarely consider the same individual over long periods of time. My own work on myself has demonstrated the existence of plateaux, and I have no reason to believe that I am unique in this regard. It seems to me quite a natural feature of learning, and I remember it well in my younger days when I was learning to play table tennis, and most especially when I was learning to fence. Research by psychologists into learning to type have shown the existence of such a plateau, and that a significant change in learning occurs when the typist progresses from a 'letter habit' to a 'word habit'.

The message to be drawn from these comments is, not to be discouraged when you feel that some lower limit has been reached. This limit is not immutable, it is not an absolute limit. In all probability, it signifies that you have reached a plateau, and that a change in your approach is almost certainly called for if you wish to progress further. In this regard, the use of the imagination, as outlined in the next chapter, will play a vital role.

# 5
# USING YOUR IMAGINATION

The imagination is a very underrated human facility in this modern age. We all have imaginations, but some people have cultivated theirs to a high degree, whilst others have relegated theirs almost to oblivion. Imagination is the mental faculty of forming images of external objects not present to the senses. More than just the object, it may also involve sensations which the object would convey. For instance, we may imagine that we are lying on a beach in the sun and can smell the salt water, feel the warm breeze and hear the birds singing – when in fact we are sitting in a chair with our eyes closed. We may imagine that we are successful, rich and popular. How to improve your imagination and how to employ it in hypnosis is very important. Your success in self-hypnosis, although not absolutely dependent on imagination, will be greater if the imagination is used.

In the first section, I shall say more about the imagination and its role in hypnosis. The following section will deal with pictorial imagination. This is very important. Before language, there were just symbols and gestures. It is very significant that, in the majority of our dreams, words and language play a very minor role, while pictures play a very dominant role. I shall illustrate, therefore, the importance of pictorial images in obtaining responses in hypnotic trances. It will be found that such a facility has a major role in non-medical uses of hypnosis which shall be discussed in Part II of this book.

In the last section, I shall return to the point about involvement, either directly or indirectly, in the form of a bystander or observer. We dealt with this, both in Chapter 1 and in Chapter 3, when we discussed dissociation. Here, I intend to stress the role of the imagination in this process. Having done this, the idea of 'the Guru within' will be discussed: our personal and wise guru whom we can consult whenever the need arises.

## The Importance of The Imagination

The success of hypnosis rests very much on being able to abandon reality-testing, i.e. on not questioning your existence in a given environment. The mind, in particular the left brain, when it receives sensory input, takes this information and compares it with information that it already has stored about the environment. If, for instance, you are in a room with a TV set which you then switch on, the brain considers the information and decides that it is acceptable: that it conforms to 'reality'. If, however, when you switched on the TV set and a person came out of the screen, then you would not accept this: you would surmise it is 'unreal'. But why? Based on past information and experience you know that this is not possible and so, if it happens, you must be imagining it – you would probably consider yourself ill!

The important point about what has just been said is that the *conscious* mind, and only the conscious mind (the left brain), undertakes the job of reality-testing. The left brain critically assesses all incoming sensory information and compares it with what knowledge it has accumulated in the past. To summarize: the conscious mind (the left brain) undertakes reality-testing, the unconscious mind (the right brain) does not. Imagination is a feature of the right brain.

This is clear from the illustration we gave above. If you are sitting in a chair, then that is the reality and there is no escaping it. (This view, however, defines 'reality' in terms of the environment in which your physical body resides, and not in relation to where your mind – unconscious mind – resides. Which is the 'true reality'?) But close your eyes and imagine that you are on a beach, which is not all that difficult; then, you must suspend criticism, you must not compare your physical location with where you imagine yourself to be. If this can be done, then during these periods the only 'reality' is that which you conjure up in your imagination. If you find this difficult, you must practise if you wish to become proficient at self-hypnosis.

Try to remember back to your childhood, when your imagination was very good. Failing that, observe children playing and see how they use their imaginations so effectively. Many children readily hallucinate, but are conditioned not to 'see' by parents by being repeatedly told that nothing is there, and so this ability, (a natural feature of the right brain) is soon forgotten. It is unfortunate that, as we get older and 'put away those childish things', we also put away our imaginations too. Imagination is not a childish thing, it is a feature of the human nervous system which is grossly under-utilized. In this chapter, my aim is to show you how you may re-learn that which you once possessed, in abundance, in your youth.

But why is the imagination so important? When we suspend reality-testing and use only our right brain, then the mind takes as 'reality' that which is suggested to it. In hypnosis, your left brain is shut down to a large extent and so reality-testing is not undertaken during hypnosis, if the depth is sufficient enough. If, then, you suggest to yourself that you are on a beach in the warm sun, lying very relaxed, etc., then the right brain will take that to *be* 'reality' and your body will accordingly respond. You become more relaxed, you feel warm, and so on. The clearer you can imagine the scene, the more success you will have in creating the feeling of warmth and relaxation. The point of great importance to note, is that the body responds physiologically to the sensations, which correspond to the situation you are creating in your imagination. A more striking illustration, in terms of the response, is to imagine that you are running a race. Your heart beat will quicken and your breathing will get deeper. These responses which occur in the hypnotic state are different from the situation of 'day-dreaming' which, to some extent, involves imagery with no physiological changes.

Once it is realized that our body, and often our actions,

respond to the things we conjure up in our imagination, then we immediately realize the force and power of the imagination. Phobias (excessive fears) are also products of imagination. Given, then, that imagination acts as a powerful force, we also must realize that it can act as either a positive force or a negative force. The common suggestion, to think and act positively, is one which you should take particular note of. Imagine you are successful, and success will come (by this, though, we do not mean 'day-dream'). The 'power of positive thinking' is no more than a restatement of: 'Faith can move mountains'. In whatever way it is phrased, the message is true. The hypochondriac is the typical negative thinker who imagines they are ill from one ailment or another. They believe it, and such belief may even bring it about, but it is a negative mental state created by destructive negative images.

In the sections to follow, I shall not be giving any negative suggestions. It is, however, important for the self-hypnotist to recognize these forces when they occur in his thinking, so that they can be eliminated. The various uses of hypnosis in character improvement, shall be discussed in Chapter 9. In order to recognize the power of negative thoughts and imaginings, I have included below just *one* involving fear. This should be attempted so that you can learn from it, or something milder, like anger. It is included only to bring to your awareness the destructive nature of negative thoughts and hence, the importance of eliminating them.

The main rule in using the imagination is to be truly imaginative. Suppose you wish to have the feeling of warmth and relaxation. You could simply suggest this to yourself. It will work, to a degree, because we respond to the words and the mind calls on past experiences associated with these words. But this is unimaginative. We have already mentioned lying in the sun on a beach. The importance of this is that the scene enhances the sensations in many respects. You may find that you picture rocks with the waves gently lapping, seagulls in the clear blue sky, and so on. The more vivid the image, the greater your response. But it need not be a beach. Sitting on the couch in front of a log fire with a brandy to warm your inside may be your idea of warmth, comfort and bliss. Then imagine this. I shall expand on such pictorial scenes in the next section.

The more outlandish your images, the more impact they have. Consider any of your dreams. Are they not outlandish? The mind, the unconscious mind that is, does not deal in words in general, but rather in symbols and pictures: pictures that contain a message or an emotion. So when you use your imagination, do the same. For those who like science fiction, arrive on some distant planet and create a scene or situation that elicits the things you want. In the above case of warmth and relaxation, for instance, imagine arriving on a planet which is beautiful, a paradise, with a warm sun (not too hot), a place of fantastic beauty and serenity. You lie down and the fragrances from the flowers transport you into a deep relaxed sleep, etc. The simple, but important point being made is to be imaginative, be outlandish.

## Pictorial Imagination

We have just referred to the importance of picturing scenes which elicit the effect you want. These should take the form of pictures. Suppose, for instance, you are suggesting that your eyelids are stuck tightly together, so that it is impossible for you to open them. Then imagine that they have been glued; *see* the glue being plastered on your eyelids in your mind's eye. Or alternatively, imagine a zip across your eyes which has been pulled too. Often images simply materialize in your awareness. These are the ones to use because they are personal and they are ones your own psyche will respond to. Take my own case. After a few attempts at this exercise I found, on repeated occasions, an image of my eyelids closed and a small man on the eyes, struggling to open them without any success – the sort of image used frequently in Walt Disney cartoons.

Take the case of your arm becoming heavy. Do not simply repeat: 'My arm is becoming heavier and heavier'; imagine that it is made of lead – see it made of lead in your imagination. Similarly, when making suggestions that your arm is becoming light, consider that your wrist is attached to a big balloon which is beginning to rise and is pulling your arm up as it rises. Or that your arm has been filled with helium gas, like the large air balloons, and will accordingly rise. It does not really matter what the image is, so long as, *in your view*, the image has the response you are seeking.

Reconsider the deepening exercises given in Chapter 3. There, a number of them could be well enhanced by using pictorial scenes. Going down the escalator is a case in point. Choose an escalator in a store or subway you know particularly well, so that you can picture it clearly. See the floors, the items on each floor: the drapery section, women's wear, men's wear, and so on. Try to imagine yourself in the store or subway in every sense – see it, feel it, hear it and even smell it. This is especially true if you use a garden scene with stairs down to a pool. Smell the roses, feel the freshness, and hear the birds.

As a full instruction and a useful one for relaxation, consider the following suggestions. The numbers once again refer to comments following the instructions:

### Pictorial Scene for Relaxation

[Name] you are in a forest in which you are making your way to a mineral spring, a familiar mineral spring (1), and you reach it and you are there, all alone. You undress and slip into the warm water. The water is soothing and is relaxing all of your muscles (2). You can feel the beneficial effects of the minerals which are passing through all parts of your skin, and into your body. And as the minerals enter your body, they are relaxing all the muscles, large and small. You can feel the soothing freshness on your face (3).

And you are now getting out, slowly, feeling very relaxed and just wanting to lie down. And so you lie down in the warm sun, the warm rays shining on your body and mixing with globules of mineral water, relaxing you still further, and sending you into a beautiful deep sleep, not a natural sleep, but a deep hypnotic sleep. Becoming all the time more and more relaxed, and deeper and deeper asleep. Everything is utterly peaceful and tranquil (4).

(1) The more you use this suggestion, the more familiar will become the mineral spring. Picture it in full. See its surroundings, the colours, whether there is a waterfall there, (although it is best to consciously introduce one). Make the whole scene so familiar that it becomes your private place for rest, relaxation and the gaining of inner strength. And that is exactly what it will become to you. After using this instruction

a few times, you will simply have to imagine the place and you will immediately elicit the relaxation and warmth in your body, without having to repeat the instructions at all – a picture is worth a thousand words. This scene is a very good preliminary to that which we shall discuss in a later section, with regard to the 'guru within'.

(2) Imagine yourself taking handfuls of water and rubbing your arms and face, and other parts of the body not in the water. See yourself ducking or swimming if you like.

(3) It is most important, both here and earlier in the scene, to actually feel the water. Feel the water on your face. Let the feeling be one of luxuriousness, as if the minerals were giving you a tingling feeling as they entered your skin and into your muscles.

(4) You can keep up these suggestions, but you should find, by this stage, that you are extremely relaxed.

You could, in fact, continue the above scene with a very vivid deepening sequence as follows:

### Pictorial Deepening
And as you are lying there looking up at the sky you are going deeper and deeper. And the day turns into night, but you are so relaxed you don't want to move. And the night is warm also and you can see the stars in the sky. And you are going deeper still. In fact you are going to go considerably deeper with each day and each night that passes.
And now the day returns once again, warm and pleasant. And now the night. Dark but warm. And the night turns into day, and you are going deeper and deeper all the time.
[Just keep this up for a while.]

This can be most effective in deepening the state. The passing of the days and nights can pick up speed, which will increase the sense of deepening. When you have the scene clearly in mind, you can dispense with words altogether. Once the stimulus-response cycle is set in motion, the deepening will occur without any words. This allows the right brain to take a still more dominant role in the deepening and allows the left brain to shut down even more.

The whole scene, both the relaxation at the mineral spring and the deepening, is one which builds up the feelings to be elicited. In one sense, the whole suggestion is no more than to relax and go deeper asleep. But, like a dream, it establishes this response by means of a series of pictorial scenes. The mineral water leads to expectancy, and the lying in the sun finally sets the scene which will elicit the feeling of relaxation that is required. The continued deepening is then associated with something that you can sense quite readily in your mind's eye.

This present method of using the imagination is far superior to the bland suggestion: 'You are relaxed and going deeper asleep,' even if this phrase is repeated many times. By using the imagination as just demonstrated, you direct all your attention to this and this alone. The more elaborate the scene, the more impossible it is for your mind to be thinking about anything else. Your attention is where you are directing it, and all your senses are being directed at achieving the one desired end. You are bound to succeed.

I said I would consider a brief negative suggestion involving fear. In doing this, I shall be calling into the imagination a non-poisonous spider. If you are really afraid of spiders, I strongly advise you not to attempt this, and replace it with some scene that makes you very angry instead. I shall suppose you are lying or sitting down.

### Negative Pictorial Suggestion
[Name] on your right leg there is a large ugly spider, big and black with hairy legs and you can see it very clearly and you can feel it on your right leg. And it's beginning to make its way up your leg towards your body ...

I think by now you get the message. The more vivid your imagination, the more you will respond to this suggestion. You will eventually flick the spider off, but not until you have felt a definite response. You should get a feeling of tenseness and your breathing may become more pronounced and your heartbeat a little faster; all are typical physiological responses in a situation of fear. When this exercise is complete, therefore, *without fail*, go through a suggestion of relaxation and calm and cancel all negative effects.

In obtaining practice at using the imagination, and it does require practice, you should conjure up scenes, as elaborate as you like, with each emphasizing one particular bodily sensation. The typical list of sensations that you should practise on are: (1) visual, (2) auditory, (3) tactual, (4) thermal, (5) olfactory, (6) kinesthetic (i.e. movement) and (7) gustatory. In general, scenes will combine a number of these. In the remainder of this section, I shall illustrate some of these by means of three instructions. The first is a desert scene, and illustrates a mixture of thermal and gustatory; the second is largely visual and kinesthetic; and the third is auditory and tactual. They are chosen particularly for the aid they will give in the uses of hypnosis to be discussed in Part II of this book. They should, accordingly, be practised by the self-hypnotist – not because of the feelings that they elicit, but as exercises in developing and extending the capacities of the right brain.

### Desert Scene

[Name] you are in the desert, the sun is beating down and it's very hot and dry. You are without water, since you used up the last of your water some hours ago. And you are very thirsty, very thirsty indeed. The sun is hot and your mouth is dry and your lips are parched. Hour after hour you are walking over the sand dunes and becoming more and more thirsty, your mouth more and more parched.

[You can continue this saga until the full effect is felt. You can, however, obtain the full impact of suggestion by continuing in the following manner.]

You now reach an oasis with palm trees and a pool. Yes, you now reach the pool and drink the cool clear water. It's so refreshing (pause). And now you sit or lie by a palm tree, relaxing in the warm sun and the day passes into evening, but you are so relaxed you just want to lie there, undisturbed.

Notice that this whole scene is no more than saying that you are hot and thirsty. You could suggest this repeatedly, and you may begin to feel a little parched and begin to swallow. But the above imagery is far more effective.

The next illustration is very good for obtaining a sense of body image. We all have a sense of our own bodies but we do not give it much conscious thought. In this exercise, the intention is to make the body first small, then tall, then finally solid. Like most of the exercises used in this book, this one, in itself, is not useful. It is its simplicity which is important and the fact that, by distorting the body image, you realize that it is possible to utilize this in other spheres, such as sport.

### Body Image

You are in the garden, lying there, feeling pleasantly relaxed. Suddenly the garden appears to be getting bigger and bigger, and the trees are getting taller and taller, and then you realize that it is not the garden that is getting bigger and the trees taller, but that you are getting smaller and smaller. Smaller still and still smaller. Three feet, two feet, one foot. You can see everything growing large and towering. And now you are the size of Tom Thumb. You see everything around you from this perspective, and the feeling of being the size of Tom Thumb is getting stronger and stronger (pause).
[Let time pass sufficiently to get a feel for the situation. Then continue.]
And now you are getting bigger and bigger. Yes, you are returning easily and quickly to your normal height. But you are continuing to grow still taller and taller. Very large, you grow taller and bigger. The house and garden are like a doll's house as you are a giant above them all. Tall strong and powerful (pause).
[After the feeling has had a chance to be felt, continue as follows.]
You are now shrinking, becoming smaller once again. Returning to your own height, to your former self, easily and quickly. Yes, you are now back to normal (pause).
And now you are feeling like stone, like a statue, very solid. Just like stone. And this feeling of being solid, just like a statue, is getting stronger and stronger. Stronger all the time (pause). And now you are returning to normal, quickly and easily. All your feelings have now returned to normal.

When this is done for the first time, it can be very startling. There is absolutely nothing to worry about in carrying out this exercise. You may dissociate fairly readily during it, without explicitly suggesting to do so. Furthermore, it is likely to have the effect of taking you deeper, again without explicitly suggesting it. This particular set of instructions should be practised by the self-hypnotist, because you will undoubtedly become more proficient at it with practice.

The first part of the body image instruction can be used as a means to dissociate. The basic means of doing this is to continue the suggestions of getting smaller until you get so small that you simply disappear! Again, there is nothing to worry about in doing this, but it can be very effective.

In all the suggestions given so far, we have supposed you remained sitting or lying with your eyes closed continuously throughout. It is now time to give a suggestion where you open your eyes. On this occasion, we shall make this only brief. With practice, you can increase the length of time the eyes remain open. Opening the eyes has a tendency to lighten the hypnotic state, so that this requires practice. In this period when you open your eyes, you will place a record on your record player. The object in this set of instructions is to actually *feel* the music. This can be a very powerful experience and, at the same time, a very fulfilling one. Here, it will be assumed that you are using 'I' for the person giving the instructions, and your personal name for the person responding.

### 'Feeling' Music

In a moment, [name], I am going to ask you to open your eyes. When you open your eyes you are still going to remain hypnotized. Having your eyes closed is not essential when you are hypnotized, but is very useful. And when you open your eyes, you will go and put on a record, which you have already chosen. And when you hear the music, you are going to hear it more intensely than you have ever heard it before. More than that, you are going to feel the music, as if all your nerve endings all over your body are responding to the music. Yes, you are going to feel the music very intensely and in a way you never thought was possible, but is. And it is going to be a most pleasant experience.

Now open your eyes, [name], and put on the record.

Once the record has been put on, you can return to your

former position and close your eyes once again and just 'feel' the music. It is best when doing this exercise to put on some orchestrated music that involves no singing. Anything that you particularly like, and on this occasion it need not be slow or quiet. The more familiar you are with the piece, the better, because you will experience it more intensely and more completely than you have ever done before. The difference will be more noticeable to you, the more familiar you are with it.

This exercise can be adapted in a number of ways, depending on the music. You may suggest that you will picture movement or any image that the music seems to signify. The right brain is very responsive to music and will almost certainly throw up images into your consciousness if these are suggested – and even when they are not suggested. A record that conjures up a storm can be most effective. The best of all, is anything in the past, vocal or not, which sends a 'shiver up your spine'. Under hypnosis, such pieces can send a bolt of energy from the base of your spine right into your brain. It can be a most dramatic and invigorating experience.

## Involvement

Since we have dealt with this to some extent, we can be brief. In the above suggestions, *you* are the person going down the escalator, *you* are the one in the mineral pool, and *you* are the one in the desert. In other words, *you* are the active participant in these scenes. This is how it should be. Your dreams are like this, (although you usually participate in them on more than one level). If you are going to elicit some feeling, then *you* need to be the person involved.

Some people find being directly involved not as easy as we have made out above. The reason is difficult to understand, but we can obtain some understanding of this by experiments done on hypnotic subjects and the relationship established between hypnosis and personality. We did this in Chapter 1 when we discussed people's involvement when reading a novel. As mentioned there, some people identify themselves with the hero or heroine and become that person, with all their fears, joys, etc. The same happens with films. Some people become so emotionally involved, that they can finish a novel or come out of a film feeling emotionally drained. Many a woman has come out of the film *Gone With the Wind*, having identified strongly with Scarlett O'Hara. This, in itself, is a form of self-hypnosis.

Other people, however, cannot do this. What they do instead, is to become observers or bystanders. It is as if they watch the scene from above: they are present but are not directly affected by it. This situation can be most useful in hypnotherapy, where a person does not wish to act something out because it is too emotionally charged and unpleasant. They may find, in this situation that they can observe the event with emotional detachment.

Such individuals who find direct involvement difficult, but being an observer manageable, can utilize the following technique: You can see yourself being hypnotized by a professional hypnotist. See yourself in the chair, see and hear the hypnotist giving you instructions; see yourself responding very well – and that is what will happen. We have already mentioned this when we discussed dissociation, but what we are adding now is a more vivid scene. Bring into the scene as many of your senses as possible. If the hypnotist is not you, then make sure it is a person who you feel you can trust absolutely, (and such a person need not exist). Picture the hypnotist in detail, most especially the voice. Feel that you must carry out all his or her suggestions – and so you will.

One person that I once hypnotized, found going deeper rather difficult, until she imagined that she was reading a novel and in this novel she was reading about a hypnotist hypnotizing the heroine. In this way, the deepening progressed. The message is, to find out in what manner you become involved and then utilize this in the most imaginative way you can.

## The Guru Within
This may seem a strange title, but it is a very apt one. Holistic medicine is becoming more widespread, especially in the United States. One feature of this approach is that the body has a tremendous capacity to heal itself. In some therapies, there is a basic principle of trying to solve your problems by 'talking it out with yourself'. Here, you place two chairs facing each other. You sit in one and imagine you are talking to

yourself in the other. You ask a question, switch chairs, and then reply. Notice, in particular, how similar this is to dissociation. It is also possible to combine these two ideas and improve the results, by using visual imagery under hypnosis.

The idea is basically simple. You imagine in your mind's eye some person, a guru (which just means wise teacher). This person does not have to be someone living or someone you know or have seen. The idea is to create an image that you consider is the symbol and essence of all wisdom. It is best to avoid the idea of God, because you need to be able to picture the person as clearly as possible. It can be male or female. The guru is someone who is personal to you and to be shared with nobody else. He or she will be available whenever you consult them, and you have absolute faith in their wisdom.

At this point, there is no need of hypnotism. But the idea is to conjure up such a person during a hypnotic session. Why? Because the wisdom that the guru is to propound is no more than your right brain supplying information to your left brain, and this can occur most easily in a hypnotic state (or in meditation). To make the whole thing more effective, it is best to always locate the guru in the same place, in surroundings with which you will become more and more familiar. Earlier, we discussed the image of the mineral pool. It is just such a place that you should conjure up, where you can always find your guru waiting. What matters is that it is a personal place which is quiet and tranquil, so that you can talk to this very wise person totally undisturbed.

I shall not present any specific image because you should work on this yourself for a while until you arrive at one that you are satisfied with. Once this occurs, do not change either the place or the guru. The purpose of creating a guru is not necessarily to deal with psychological disorders, although this can be done, but to help in making important decisions. An important decision leads to anxiety and anxiety leads to tension, which together seem to make decisions difficult to make. In a relaxed hypnotic state, decisions can be considered more objectively. Consulting your own guru can be better still. It is the basis of asking any religious deity to help you to make the right decision. You need not be religious, but simply realize that we have more within ourselves than we normally admit to.

## Conclusion

Imagination is not something you have or do not have. It is something we all have – but to different degrees. Those people with little imagination have weakened this facility of the right brain, through lack of use. It has to be re-learned and utilized repeatedly during hypnosis. Its value cannot be stressed sufficiently.

In Part II, I shall turn to a number of non-medical situations in which self-hypnosis can help and, in each case, particular attention will be given to the role of the imagination. So, practice in the early stages will carry through into the future. Never lose the opportunity to practise and develop your imagination.

This concludes the formal aspects of hypnosis. The exercises should be practised, as exercises, so that they can develop those aspects of the right brain which can be used to help you in various ways. The dominance of the left brain in mental activity has led man to under-utilize his full potential. It is hoped that, with the means of self-hypnosis, the individual can call on the energy and potential that is there waiting within himself or herself. How this energy can be used in non-medical situations is the subject matter of Part II.

# PART II

# THE NON-MEDICAL USES OF SELF-HYPNOSIS

# 6
# RELAXATION THROUGH SELF-HYPNOSIS

In this day and age, people do not know how to relax. 'A change is as good as a rest' is only a half truth. A change is therapeutic and rekindles interest in things, but it is not relaxing. To relax, in a strict sense, is to be totally inactive, a process of letting the muscles go completely and to eliminate all possible tension in them. This is no easy task, although it can be, with some practice. The first problem, however, is to recognize the tension that we already have in our muscles.

We have already pointed out that the induction routine, outlined in Chapter 2, is one of progressive relaxation. Anyone who has already embarked on self-hypnosis will notice the difference in body tension. The early stages of hypnosis are generally replete with suggestions of limpness, relaxation and going deeper asleep. The repetition will enhance this effect. But even more gain can be made by learning to relax even more. This requires practice. It is true that when we are anxious, then relaxing relieves this. But it is no good leaving the moment to learn relaxation until we are anxious – it is better to learn to swim before you fall in the sea! The aim is to cultivate the *habit* of relaxing and being able to achieve it at a given conscious stimulus: to make relaxation part of our nervous system, so that it is conditioned and can respond immediately when the need arises. That is the aim of this chapter. Relaxation is to be built into the nervous system, so that it becomes automatic, so that we can bring it about with a conscious signal when we want it and when we need it most.

Basically, this chapter will deal with the use of self-hypnosis as a means of achieving relaxation. Second, I shall discuss the use of post-hypnotic suggestions for relaxation during the day or during some particularly anxious moments, such as an interview or some public function. Before this, however, the first section gives some general points about how tension manifests itself in the body. Only through such knowledge can you tackle the problem head-on.

## Tension in the Body

Whenever a muscle is being used it will contract, it will exhibit 'tension'; when a muscle is not being exerted, then it will lengthen and 'relax'. Throughout this chapter, the term 'relaxation' will refer to the absence of tension in the muscles. This is a very specific usage, but an important one to understand. When you relax, in the sense used here, you do not make an effort to do so, you simply do nothing. By doing nothing, the muscles will elongate on their own. *Relaxation is simply the absence of tension.* This is very important, you cannot make an effort to relax, because to do so means that some muscle or muscles will contract and will exhibit tension. To repeat, relaxation is the absence of tension. Put simply, it is 'letting go'.

Because we so rarely 'let go', it is something which has to be practised. More importantly, we often think that we are relaxed when we are not. But how do we know this? First, by recognizing what tension feels like and then continuing to relax beyond the point we have already reached. Given the tensions of modern society, it is almost certain that if you consider yourself fully relaxed, you are not; more can be achieved. Assume, throughout, that at all times even greater relaxation is possible. This working hypothesis will undoubtedly pay dividends.

There is a theory concerning residual tension, to which the present writer subscribes, which is that it remains in the muscles and builds up over long periods of time. Let me put it in the following way. Suppose you become angry and you shout, or whatever. Some of the tension is dissipated in the shouting, but not all. Assume, for the moment, that this is the case. Then the obvious question to ask is: 'What happens to the remainder?' In fact, it is absorbed. Generally, we do not engage in pursuits which eliminate this residual. Notice, in this argument, that not to give vent to one's tension requires the intervention of the ego; the left brain must impose a constraint on allowing the pleasure principle of the id to manifest itself. In time, there is a culmination of such tension which builds up in the muscles, especially in the muscles of the stomach. I am not, of course, suggesting that you should shout longer and louder! What I am suggesting is that we have much residual tension which builds up in our muscles and requires to be eliminated by one means or another. Exercise is a good method, and the popularity of hatha yoga, based, as it is, on exercise, can be most therapeutic.

If this theory concerning residual tension is correct, then we have had many years to accumulate such tension in the muscles, which cannot be eliminated, either quickly or easily, with just a few days' attention. Even if we pay attention to this problem from the present onwards, we shall only cope with our immediate tensions and still leave the tensions which have accumulated from the past. We will have to deal with these accumulated tensions. But how?

In attempting to do this, we must establish exactly *what* makes us tense, second, establish *where* in the body such tension manifests itself. This is quite a tall order, but the effort will more than pay dividends. Whenever you become tense, make a mental note of what it is that is causing the tension. By this I do not mean, say, when your child does something naughty you become annoyed and tense. Don't blame others. What must be ascertained is why such behaviour on the part of the child makes *you* tense. It is *your* behaviour which is under the microscope, not the child's. If you cannot pin down the reason precisely, then take a note of the situation in which it occurs. If possible, write these down so that you can catalogue them to see if there is any common pattern. Next make a mental note, or again write it down, *where* the tension occurs in your body. Is it in your face? Is it in the stomach? Is it in your back? And so on. If you never give this any conscious thought, (i.e. bring your left brain to bear on what is basically created in your right brain – your unconscious mind), then you cannot possibly begin to eliminate the tension. It is most important that you establish why you become tense and where your tension manifests itself in the body.

During one or more of your self-hypnotic sessions, just reflect on these. Since you are fairly relaxed when you are in a hypnotic state, you will find such self-appraisal easier and more objective than if you did it in your normal waking state. The deeper you go, the more you will ascertain, because the more likely your answer, in whatever form it comes, will arise from your unconscious mind: and the unconscious does not lie – it may misdirect, as it does in dreams, but that is a different story. The message of this section is that you must take the learning of relaxation seriously. It must be learned and practised and, with practice, it will become easier, quicker and more successful.

## Self-Hypnosis and Relaxation

The art of using self-hypnosis for relaxation falls into two main categories. First, a thorough repetition of relaxation and limpness, going from head to toe and then back again. Here, the aim is to work progressively on every muscle, large and small, especially muscles in the face and the back of the neck. The second, is to use imagery to create the relaxation. In this section, we shall concentrate on this second aspect.

The point to remember is that when you are hypnotized and create a relaxing scene, the unconscious mind takes this to be reality, and so sends messages to the rest of your body to act accordingly. The stronger the image, the more effective your results. Take the following as an example:

### Relaxation 1: The Sauna and Massage

[Name], you are going into a sauna lounge. You have a sauna which relaxes all your muscles. You are lying in the room, letting the warmth pass all over and through your body and, as it does so, it takes away all your tensions, all your stiffness away from your body, and you begin to feel much more relaxed and less and less tense. And the warm air is relaxing all parts of your

body, from the tips of your toes to the top of your head.
And, [name], you come out of the sauna and lie down on your
stomach, letting yourself relax ready to be massaged. And the
masseur begins with your shoulders, relaxing the muscles of
your shoulders and your neck. Removing still more of that
tension. And now he begins to work on your back and on your
arms, rubbing and massaging away all the remaining tension.
And as he does so, so you are feeling much more relaxed and
are going into a still deeper sleep, more limp and relaxed as the
massage continues.

[Keep this up for as long as you want. Elaborate the scene if you
like.]

For those people who have had a massage done, especially by a
professional, you should call to mind such an experience
when you are making these suggestions. In this way, you will
feel the experience and so make it more effective. You do not,
of course, have to be in a sauna. The point is to create a typical
scene where relaxation is both expected and natural.

To illustrate the diversity of mental images for creating
relaxation consider this next one:

### Relaxation 2: The Log Cabin

[Name], you are up in the mountains, out in the snow and it's
very cold, a blizzard is blowing and you are making your way to
your log cabin. You arrive at the cabin and go in. You are alone
and it is very warm because a log fire has been burning for
some time. You take off your outer clothes and go over to the
fire to warm yourself.

You are quite warm now and you undress and put on
something soft and light. And you take a glass of brandy. You
can feel the warmth of the fire and the warmth of the brandy.
And you are sitting now warm and cosy, looking into the
flames, feeling utterly relaxed and peaceful. And the mixture
of the warm fire and the brandy is making you feel very
relaxed, very sleepy and you are going down into a deep
hypnotic sleep. And as you stare into the flames and feel so
warm and secure, so you sink down into a deeper and more
relaxed sleep than you ever thought possible.

The success of this set of suggestions rests very much on your imagery and how involved and pleasant you can make the scene. For instance, you may wish to unclothe totally and lie down in front of the fire on a beautifully soft lamb carpet. Or you may wish to introduce into the scene a dog, who is already sleeping peacefully at the fireside, and you lie down beside it. The object, in all cases, is to make the scene pleasing and one that *you* particularly find so. Practise a few variants until you find one that you clearly respond to.

It is possible to combine music with relaxation. This is best done with a tape that switches itself off when it comes to the end. But the important point is to find music that *you* feel will be relaxing. You know your own taste in music, but it should be orchestral or a solo instrument. It should be one that moves your imagination to the sea, the sky and vast open spaces. Some people find Ravel's *Bolero* useful for this; although others find the repetition of its basic theme jars their sensibilities, and so they become restless instead. The music should certainly not be lively, since this will stimulate you, rather than enhance relaxation. Once the music has been selected, then relaxation suggestions can be combined with whatever mood the music suggests.

## Post-Hypnotic Suggestions and Relaxation

Many people find that their job or circumstances are such that they become very tense during the day. Others find that particular occasions or functions are very stressful, leading to anxiety. These are clearly particular to you, but all of them have the same ingredient – tension. A major use of post-hypnotic suggestion is the reduction of tension in these situations.

Let me take a particular illustration. Suppose you are to give a public lecture or talk at some evening get-together. Most people would find that they are apprehensive about such a prospect, and this leads to tension. Tension leads to worry and the idea of a poor performance, which leads to even more tension, so setting up a vicious circle. The object of the hypnotic session is two-fold. The first is to mentally picture the scene, while in a relaxed hypnotic state, in such a way that you are giving the best performance of your life. The second objective is to tell yourself that, on the occasion it actually does occur, you will be equally relaxed and will give an equally impressive performance. The suggestions may go something like this:

### Elimination of Tension Prior to Some Engagement

[Name], tomorrow night (or whenever), you are going to be giving a talk to ... You can already picture yourself in the room on the platform (or at the dinner table), and you are calm relaxed and confident. Yes, [name], you can picture yourself, very clearly, being extremely relaxed and confident.

You now stand and give the most relaxed talk, and it is the best performance you have ever given. Your talk is natural because you are very relaxed. You are not tense, either in your body or in your voice.

[Try to picture yourself as clearly as possible, above all in a very relaxed and confident manner.]

You speak clearly and confidently. You are informative, interesting, amusing, [or whatever is appropriate]. The whole audience can see this, and you warm to the whole affair very quickly indeed. You see that there is nothing to worry about and your talk goes down exceptionally well.

After the talk, you meet other people and they congratulate you on how well they enjoyed your talk.

Believe absolutely in this and in the scene you are creating. Fill the whole scene with feelings of relaxation, composure and confidence – exaggerate if necessary. The stronger the image, the more likely it will be carried out. You now continue with a post-hypnotic suggestion, which is to come into force at the moment you are at the engagement.

### Post-hypnotic Suggestion for a Forthcoming Engagement

[Name], just as you have now been relaxed when delivering the talk, confident and relaxed, so then will you be that way tomorrow evening when you come to give your talk. Yes, tomorrow evening you will be just as relaxed, just as confident as you have been a moment ago. Yes, [name], tomorrow you will be equally confident and equally relaxed. Your talk is going to be just as you have imagined it to be. And, most especially, you are not going to be concerned about it between now and then. You are going to treat it simply as another thing to be done. The last thing you want to do, the last thing you will do, is worry about it. In fact, there is no need for worry, because you know absolutely that you are going to be very relaxed and confident and give the best talk of your life.

The object is to embellish the scene, fill it with positive and confident thoughts and actions. Repeat it as often as seems necessary, but with slight variations, so that you do not become bored. Of course, you can repeat such suggestions over a few days up to the time of the talk. Try, however, not to give the talk too much attention because this will indicate that you are worried about it. Simply treat the talk as something interesting and to be looked forward to.

Another useful post-hypnotic suggestion, which can be constantly used, is the use of a single word to 'trigger' in you a feeling of relaxation, whenever and wherever you use it. The advantage of this is that the more frequently it is used, the more likely you will establish a stimulus-response reaction. The obvious word to use is 'relax', although any word will do that *you* can associate with relaxation. It may, for instance, be the word 'Greece' if this conjures up a fantastic, relaxing holiday you had in Greece. Whatever the word, it should have as powerful an association with relaxation as possible. You can then employ the following post-hypnotic suggestion:

**Post-hypnotic Cue Word to Bring About Relaxation**
[Name], whenever you say the word *relax*, a fantastic feeling of relaxation will spread up through your body, rising up from the floor through your toes and ascending to the top of your head. Yes, whenever you say the word *relax*, this will be a signal for you to do just that, yes, [name], you will feel a sensation of utter relaxation spreading up through the whole of your body. It will not matter whether you are standing or sitting, whenever you say the word *relax*, a feeling of utter relaxation and calm will come over you. The feeling will be very strong and powerful. So strong and powerful that it will be able to overcome any feeling of tension or anxiety that you may be feeling at that moment. Yes, [name], whenever you say the

word *relax*, a feeling of peace and calm will spread throughout the whole of your body.

And it will not matter whether you are alone or in a group, you will always find that, whenever you say to yourself *relax*, then you will do just that. Even if you are at a party and feeling tense, whenever you say the word *relax*, you will experience a feeling of utter relaxation and all signs of tension will immediately pass away and will be replaced by a feeling of calm and relaxation.

This type of post-hypnotic suggestion can usefully be put on tape and repeated frequently. The more often it is played when you are in a deep hypnotic state, the more effective it will be. Remember, however, post-hypnotic suggestions work at virtually any depth of trance and so you should not be put off if you have not yet reached a great depth of trance. That will come in time.

## Conclusion

It cannot be stressed enough that the art of relaxation must be learned and practised. The rewards from this alone are worth the effort of learning self-hypnosis.

Relaxation sessions should be engaged in frequently. The morning, before going to work, is especially beneficial. A quiet and relaxed mind and body in the morning will set the trend for the day. A lunchtime session is, beyond doubt, the most beneficial, but the one you are likely to put off the most. It need not be a long session, and can be done sitting in a chair or lying on the floor for five or ten minutes – worth thirty minutes or more at any other time of the day. There is no excuse that you cannot be alone – do it while sitting on the toilet if necessary!

A relaxation session after a hard day is also very therapeutic. Do not take a drink of alcohol or eat immediately, simply carry out a hypnotic session for about thirty minutes and this will return your energy and put you in 'full spirits' for the evening.

I cannot stress enough that relaxation, taken first thing in the morning, at lunch time and in the early evening relaxes you for the whole day, preserves your energy, strength and vitality throughout the day, and prevents you from feeling tired or worn-out. What you will be quite surprised to find is that although you spend, say, two hours in relaxation you gain anywhere up to five hours or more in productive work at other times. By that, I do not necessarily mean at your job. I mean simply, a full interest and participation in all things that you do during the day. You will find interest and enjoyment in what you do, because you will not feel tired, tense or anxious.

# 7
# DISSOCIATION

In Chapter 3, I introduced the concept of dissociation and used it as a method of deepening the hypnotic state. Let me now take this discussion of dissociation further.

As we pointed out, dissociation refers to the ability a person has to 'detach' himself from his immediate environment; of 'stepping outside' of himself and observing himself and being in other places simultaneously. We all possess this faculty and it is utilized considerably in dreams. However, as with other faculties we have discussed, people have this ability to varying degrees. But once again, it is possible to cultivate the ability with a little practice.

Dissociation is as old as man. Socrates was known to dissociate on frequent occasions, and the shamans of all ages have utilized this ability. Automatic writing, to be explained later, is also based on the ability to dissociate, but in this case, to dissociate the writing arm. Some researchers have argued that the degree of dissociation is the same as the degree of hypnosis and, accordingly, would argue that hypnosis is no more than dissociation. This is not the case, and rests on a lack of understanding, both of the phenomenon of hypnosis and that of dissociation. Many hypnotic features can be illustrated without the aid of dissociation. Furthermore, by making such a link, hypnosis becomes associated with only *one* of its

characteristics. It is like defining a bicycle as a machine with
two wheels! There is little doubt that the degree of dissociation
a person can achieve is linked, in some way, to the depth of
hypnosis a person can achieve: generally, the greater the
ability to dissociate, the greater the depth of hypnosis. In
addition, the degree of dissociation is also linked to the degree
of amnesia that can be achieved. A somnambulist who is
amnesic can usually dissociate to a very high degree. But once
again, varying degrees of dissociation can occur without
amnesia. Dissociation, therefore, is neither necessary nor
sufficient for hypnosis to occur.

One other general observation is worth making about
dissociation. Once dissociation has been established in a
hypnotic state, the person becomes much more suggestible
and instructions are much more readily absorbed by the
unconscious mind, and acted upon.

The next section will deal with three different sets of
instructions that can be used to achieve dissociation. In a later
section, I shall take up some points raised by these instructions
– including a discussion of glove anaesthesia and automatic
writing. In the following section, the relationship between
dissociation and the ego, and why, therefore, dissociation is
important in hypnotherapy, will come under discussion. As in
other chapters of this book, my intention is to deal, most
particularly, with non-medical uses of hypnosis and this
aspect will be stressed here.

## How to Achieve Dissociation

The aim of these suggestions is to 'detach' yourself from your
immediate environment, to 'step outside' of yourself. In the
first of the three instructions, I shall employ this term
somewhat literally. In the second and third instructions,
dissociation is brought about by means of pictorial images. In
each case, it is assumed that you are already in a hypnotic state.

### Dissociation 1: Stepping Out of Your Body

[Name], you are now stepping out of your body, you can feel
yourself rising from the chair. Yes, you have no difficulty in
rising up out of your body. It is as if there are two of you: the
one rising from the chair and the one remaining seated in the

chair. And this is happening now with no difficulty at all. You are stepping out of your body and moving about the room – in your mind's eye (pause).

You can see yourself sitting in the chair and you look very peaceful and very relaxed and in a deep hypnotic state. And there appears nothing strange about seeing yourself in the chair. All your consciousness seems to be with the person outside. You can see everything in the room, including yourself, very clearly indeed. And now you can give that person in the chair instructions, and he will carry them out, without any difficulty whatsoever. And you will be able to observe how well he is carrying out your suggestions.

This straightforward set of instructions can be very effective and is well worth practising. The important aspect is to have your consciousness in the person outside your body. In your normal waking state you are aware that your thoughts are in your head. This tends to localize your thoughts and contains them in the body. It is possible, however, to have them 'outside' of the body. When this is achieved, the person is said to have dissociated, and the person 'left' in the chair is more amenable to suggestion.

What seems to be happening is that your conscious awareness, which resides in the left brain, locates itself 'outside' of the body; while the physical body sitting in the chair is then controlled solely by the right brain. The dissociation is no more than operating the two hemispheres of the brain independently of one another. And why not? You have two arms and hands which look fairly alike, but are not. You rarely let one dangle unused while you concentrate on using the other. No. You achieve more by utilizing your arms and hands independently and yet in co-operation. So why not use your two brains in the same manner? It has been argued that Leonardo da Vinci had both left and right brains equally developed, which is one reason why he could write with both hands simultaneously. The obvious school game to demonstrate that, for most of us, the two halves are not equally developed, is that of rubbing your stomach with your left hand in a clockwise direction and circling your head with your right hand in a counter-clockwise direction – and then try to switch directions repeatedly.

### Dissociation 2: Disappearing

[Name], you awaken from a sound sleep, you are in bed and very comfortable. But you now feel yourself becoming smaller and smaller. You are shrinking, first to four feet, then to three feet, two feet. The bed now appears tremendously large and looks the size of a football pitch. And you continue to get smaller. Now you are only one foot tall and becoming smaller still.

And you are not, in any way, worried about this sensation or any other sensations that you may have. You will be taking a very detached interest in the whole thing.

And now you are continuing to get smaller and smaller. You are now so small, smaller than an ant, that you can move around in the fibres of the pillow or sheets. Yes, you are so small that you can crawl around the fibres which look like giant stalks (pause and really feel this experience).

And you are continuing to get smaller. You are smaller than a molecule and in fact so small that you can pass in and out of the fibre. And you now vanish altogether!

This can be a very absorbing scene and one which you may respond to in a variety of ways. There is no harm that can arise from this instruction, although, on the first occasion, the sensations which may be created can surprise you. Never be alarmed. Simply realize that no harm can come to you and just let things happen. By the time that you have vanished (!), you will be in a dissociated state. Why? Because the person becoming smaller and smaller must be some 'other' person from the one in the chair, and so the two must dissociate. The scene does not have to be a bed, it can be outdoors, or anywhere else you may like. The message is: Be imaginative.

### Dissociation 3: Change in Body-image

[Name], you are becoming very, very heavy. So heavy that you feel as though you are made of lead, and you can feel yourself sinking down into the chair as you become heavier and heavier (pause).

Now, [name], you are returning to your normal weight. You are becoming lighter and lighter. Very light indeed. As light as a feather, and still more light. And you are becoming so light that you can feel yourself rising up just a little amount (pause). Now you are returning to your normal weight, quickly and easily. And now you feel as if you are made of wood, yes you can feel yourself made of wood. You are a young tree bending and swaying in the breeze, and you can feel the wind blowing through your leaves. (pause)

And now you are becoming very porous, very porous indeed, so porous that the wind is blowing right through you. And you are expanding, expanding more and more and you *are* the wind. Yes, [name], you are now the wind, blowing over mountains and lakes. (pause)

And now [name], you are becoming a whirl-wind, yes, a whirl-wind, and you are at the centre and you are spinning faster and faster, faster and faster. So fast now that you go shooting off into space.

Once again, this can become very absorbing because you will experience a number of sensations. As the scene unfolds, you should allow enough time in the pauses to let the sensations take effect on the body. Inevitably, you will dissociate from the person in the chair. Your thoughts and your conscious awareness seems to be 'out there' in the wind and in the whirl-wind. If you have not dissociated before you become a whirl-wind, this will almost certainly bring it about. Once these instructions have been completed and you have gone off into space (!), after some moments of silence you can continue with suggestions, because now you will be in a much more suggestible state.

## Some Points About Dissociation

Having tried some, or all, of these exercises on dissociation, you will have a clear appreciation of what it means. The first observation to make about your response is that your attention is moved to the scene – whether rising out of your body, becoming smaller, or becoming a whirl-wind. Your attention is directed away from your physical body and there is a splitting of consciousness. This allows you to release the conscious hold on your physical body, which remains sitting in the chair. The right brain is then free to operate on your physical body, by means of the unconscious mind.

Far from being an act of introversion, dissociation allows you to have a clearer perspective about your body-image because you can become critical of yourself. Psychologists have demonstrated that we do have a body-image, which has been shaped by past experiences and associations with people and places. Dissociation allows you both to distort your body-image temporarily, and to take on others. This, then, gives you more of an appreciation of your own body-image. You cannot be aware of air, which is necessary for life. You can be aware of polluted air, or more significantly you can be aware of its absence, but you cannot be aware of its presence. The same tends to be true about body-image. But, unlike air, we can become aware of it by means of dissociation.

A second observation about dissociation is its use in such things as 'glove anaesthesia', i.e. the loss of feeling in the hand, or anaesthesia in other parts of the body. What is done, in these cases, is to dissociate the appropriate part of the body. Let us take glove anaesthesia as the simplest example. In this instruction, the object is to dissociate the hand. When this is done, your awareness lies 'outside' in the imagined hand and so leaves your physical hand insensitive to pain. You can only feel pain when you are aware of it, and since your awareness is 'in' the imagined hand which feels no pain, then you feel no pain. Before proceeding with the instructions, it is important first to know the location of your actual right arm, on which we shall direct attention. We shall assume, throughout, that you have both arms on the arms of the chair.

### Glove Anaesthesia

[Name], you can imagine raising your right arm until it is horizontal. You can see, in your mind's eye, your right arm held out horizontal. You can feel the tension in your horizontal arm as it stretches out straight. All your awareness is concerned with your right outstretched arm. You can see your right hand, with fingers outstretched, pointing at the wall opposite.
[Continue the image until the awareness is well established in your 'extended limb'.]

This type of suggestion is usually undertaken in a hetero-hypnotic situation. If anaesthesia can be accomplished, it has been used in operations, childbirth and dentistry. In the self-hypnotic context it can only be used as a means of redirecting your attention, your awareness, away from the source of the pain. If, however, you had a pain in your right hand, you would be better to direct your attention completely away from your hand and to something different. The point of including this is to demonstrate the importance of dissociation. All research demonstrates that pain remains present in the location, but if you can redirect your awareness, then the pain will not be felt. Dissociation is just one technique of redirecting your awareness.

The idea of dissociation in your arm is useful in another phenomenon, namely that of automatic writing. Although automatic writing can be done in a non-hypnotic state and without the aid of dissociation, it can be accomplished easier by means of hypnosis. The idea is basically the same as glove anaesthesia, but now, having dissociated your awareness away from your physical right hand, you then make suggestions to the effect that your right hand, which is now resting on a page of paper and holding a pen, is controlled solely by the unconscious mind. Thus, you prepare yourself with a board and paper on your lap and a pen resting in your right hand. You then dissociate as in glove anaesthesia, and continue the suggestions in the following manner:

### Automatic Writing
You can imagine your right arm and hand now in the air. All your awareness is in your right arm which is in the air. The right arm on the pad is going to be controlled by your unconscious mind. Yes, your awareness is on your right arm in the air but your unconscious is going to control your right arm on the pad. (pause)
And now your unconscious is making your right hand write on the paper. It is going to write whatever it wishes, whatever it feels you ought to know.

Wait a few moments. The writing may begin in a jerky fashion, it may or may not be intelligible; it may even be in the form of mirror writing. Most certainly, it could be joined together and use its own form of shorthand, e.g. to, too or two is likely to be written '2'. Basically, the right brain does not conform to the usage of English. This has begun to interest those involved in linguistics, but they must realize that 'primitive language', or what Chomsky calls 'deep structure', is a feature of the right brain and not the left, in which words and 'surface structure' is processed. In carrying out automatic writing you need not be in a hypnotic state, but you must be capable of dissociating your writing arm. This is a clear illustration of why dissociation and hypnosis are different.

A third aspect of dissociation is its relationship to fantasy. The easier you find it to fantasize, the easier you will find it to dissociate. Children like fairy stories and fantasize quite frequently. They also frequently dissociate. They do not consider this unusual, because, to them, it seems quite natural and all children do it to varying degrees – they, at least, understand what each other mean! As we 'put away childish things', so we also tend to put away fantasizing. Why this is classified as 'childish' and not 'grown up' is, in my view, a feature of our age of reason.

As reason and logic have become dominant, so we have become very left brain dominated, and so such fantasies have been demoted, simply because they do not involve reason. But the human mind is more aware of its needs than man gives it credit for, and so such tales remain. Parents rarely fail to get some personal delight when telling their children a fairy tale. This mode of expression has remained in places like India and the near East. The *Tales of a Thousand and One Nights* still has great charm for the young and old alike. The need for such (right brain) stimulus is well attested by Tolkien's *Lord of the Rings*, which required it to be classified as a 'grown up' fairy tale before it really became popular. *Star Trek*, probably the most popular TV science fiction series, was originally screened during children's hour (at least in Britain), but now has a wide adult following. Fairy tales, like science fiction, possess a charm that appeals, not to our reason, but to our imagination; not to the left brain, but to the right; not to the conscious mind, but to the unconscious mind.

## Dissociation and the Ego
It is not my intention here to become involved in a psycho-

logical debate, especially on the merits of Freudian concepts of the personality. These concepts have now become part of our common language. Freud saw personality as composed of three interrelated systems which he called the id, the ego and the superego. Briefly, the id is the original source of personality with which a child is born, including its instincts and drives. The id works according to the *pleasure principle* – it avoids pain and obtains pleasure, regardless of external considerations. The id, however, is constrained by the later developments of the ego and the superego. The ego relates the mental images with reality: it works according to the *reality principle*, which requires it to test reality and delay any bodily tensions until the appropriate environmental conditions are obtained.

The ego is realistic and logical, and its purpose is to create a plan which can be executed in the environment in which it lives, in order to achieve satisfaction. Thus the id requires immediate satisfaction, while the ego intervenes and chooses the time, the place, and which conditions are to be satisfied. The ego is the 'executor' of the id.

The superego concerns a person's values and morals. As the ego is the executor of the id, so the superego considers whether the plan of action, chosen by the ego, does not violate the values and morals of society, to which the individual belongs.

It is very important to realize that when hypnosis is achieved, we have a more direct link with the id. In addition, the superego is still operating at all times – both in the waking state and in the hypnotic state. Of course, because reality-testing has been suspended, a person can be fooled into believing something which is harmful is not really so. In other words, if the superego is fooled, then the person may carry out something which the superego would normally have not allowed. For this to occur, the person would have to be a somnambulist so that the ego is fully repressed. Furthermore, this fooling of the ego can only take place in heterohypnosis; if you are hypnotizing yourself you would not want to fool your superego.

But what has all this to do with dissociation? By dissociating, a person can become an observer – either of himself or someone else. More to the point, he can experience things that would otherwise be prevented by his ego.

To illustrate, take the case where you have to make an important decision, e.g. a change of job. You could then attempt the following experiment. After inducing hypnosis you could carry out a dissociation. Once dissociated, you can begin to ask the person in the chair about his present job; how he feels about it, what he would think about having another job, and so on. The answers, so elicited, would be those which are most 'true to your nature'. One important point must be stressed, however. It is the case that the answers are true to your nature, but because the ego has been suppressed the answers you may receive may not be feasible, given your present circumstances, i.e. they may be unrealistic. If this is the case, you will know that you will be anxious and tense, to some extent, until your true nature has full expression. For instance, it is possible that the new job pays less money, but gives you greater satisfaction. Your unconscious, freed from the ego, will allow the pleasure principle to operate freely and you may, accordingly, reply that you should take the new job. If your financial circumstances cannot afford such a move, then caution is clearly called for. If you knew you would get more satisfaction from the new job, then such a use of self-hypnosis would be uncalled for. But often we do not know how much we dislike the job we are in. Suppose, therefore, that you were considering a change of job which paid roughly the same, but involved a complete change in life-style for you and your family. It is for this type of decision that self-hypnosis and dissociation can be most useful to you.

We have already dealt with the problem of giving a public talk in Chapter 6. Seeing yourself giving such a talk in your mind's eye, means that you have already dissociated to some extent. It can be made even more effective by first dissociating. The person 'outside' who is free from all anxiety and pressure, i.e. is free from the ego, can then be seen to give the talk. The suggestion that you will do precisely the same when the event arises, is an important post-hypnotic suggestion to add. Since you have 'seen' it done and since the 'you' in the chair is separated from this other 'you', then the post-hypnotic suggestion will be more readily accepted.

The conclusion to draw from this chapter is that, for the self-hypnotist, the facility to dissociate can be used in a variety of ways, and all to your benefit.

# 8

# TIME DISTORTION

Time distortion is probably the second most important use of hypnosis, after that of relaxation, at least in terms of the non-medical uses. But what is time distortion? To explain this, a distinction must be made between clock time (or objective time) and subjective time. Clock time means what it says; namely, the time that elapses as registered by the clock. Subjective time, on the other hand, is the elapse of time that a person *perceives* has taken place.

To take some examples. Most people have experienced waiting for a bus or train, when time seems to go very slowly indeed; it may feel as though twenty or more minutes have elapsed when, by clock time, only a minute or two has passed. The same experience is felt when you cannot get to sleep. It may feel as if you have been lying there for hours, when it is in fact, no more than fifteen minutes. These are examples of *time expansion*. A different sense of time tends to occur when you are very absorbed in something, then time just seems to fly. Two or more hours, as measured by the clock, may have elapsed and yet you feel as though it has only been half-an-hour. In the morning, you awake and, on occasions, lie there for what you feel is only two minutes which, by clock time, is half-an-hour or more. These are examples of *time contraction*. Time expansion and contraction is illustrated in Figure 5.

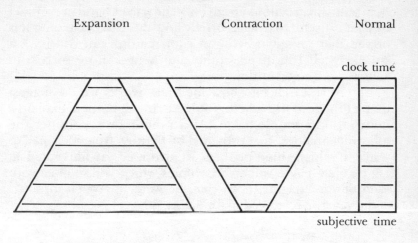

Figure 5.

These experiences are so common that people fail to see their true significance. To begin with, these examples show that subjective time and clock time are not the same thing. Given that they are not the same thing, an event can be experienced according either to clock time or to subjective time. In the examples just cited, one seems to have no control over whether you experience something by clock time or subjective time. But they do illustrate that subjective time is purely a feature of your state of mind. Once this is realized, it is but a short and significant step, to realize that subjective time can be controlled. You would never raise the question: 'How can subjective time be controlled?' unless you consider that it can, in the first instance, be subject to control. It can, and this chapter is concerned with how to control subjective time: how to expand it and how to contract it.

Because so few people are aware that subjective time can be controlled, I shall begin with a hypothetical explanation as to how it is possible to distort subjective time. This is done with the aid of a holograph, used to represent the function of the brain.

## Holographs and Time Distortion

Before any instructions are given on how to expand or contract time, it is useful to discuss briefly how this can occur, and it is hoped that, by giving you an explanation, you will have a stronger belief in its possibility and hence, more success in achieving time distortion.

Recent research into how the brain works would suggest that it functions like a holograph. Let me first, then, explain a holograph in simple terms. As a preliminary, consider the following analogy, first provided by Bentov. Imagine a pail of water in which three pebbles are dropped, as illustrated in Figure 6(a). These will create ripples which will interact with each other. Imagine, now, that the water is frozen instantly and a layer is extracted as in Figure 6(b).

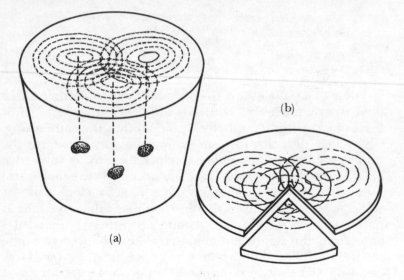

Figure 6.

Now if we take a slice of this layer, then information about *all* three pebbles is recorded, in terms of the interaction taking place in the ripples (which are now frozen). In other words, the slice does not simply record the information about the pebble in its area but also information about the other two pebbles in a different part of the layer. Each slice, as it were, has information about the whole. It is this aspect which is important in holography.

The basic idea is illustrated in Figure 7, where a hologram of an apple is being constructed. The upper part shows a laser beam which is split into two parts, one part continues until it hits the photographic plate, this is called the *reference beam*. In the lower part, consisting of the *working beam*, the beam comes into contact with an object (here an apple) before it hits the photographic plate. The two beams meet on the photographic plate and interact, forming an interference pattern – just like the frozen ice in Figure 6(b). This constitutes the hologram and it looks very much like a contour map rather than anything like a photograph of the original object. If, however, a laser is once again shone on the exposed film, an apple will appear in mid-air and with a three-dimensional appearance. Just as for the pebbles, it is the two beams which interact to form the hologram.

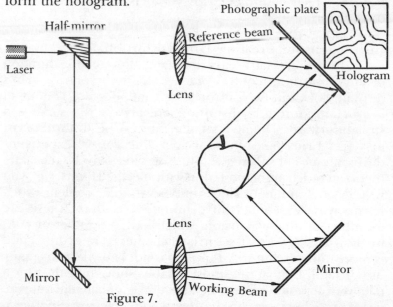

Figure 7.

In normal photography, each point on the photographic plate records only that part of the image which falls on that section. While in the holograph we see that each point of the hologram stores all the information about the object. Each point contributes more information and clarifies the object, because each point records the object from a slightly different angle.

What all this means, in the present context, is that you can perceive and experience a whole lifetime of experiences in a very short time, without any great difficulty. The famous anecdote that the dying man sees his whole life pass before his eyes in an instant of time, is a case in point. This is not as far-fetched as some people suppose. What the brain can contract, it can also expand. As shall be pointed out in Chapter 11, we tend to operate in the real world in a linear fashion. However, research based on holography would suggest that information is neither coded in the brain in a linear fashion, nor does it recall information in a linear fashion. These ideas are new at the moment and not accepted by everyone. But the holo-graphic nature of the brain would explain a number of features which have baffled psychologists, not least, that of time distortion.

## Instructions for Creating Time Distortion

Time distortion is fairly easy to obtain, although the duration of time distortion requires practice. Under hypnosis, man's in-built clock can be controlled to some degree. The initial instructions for time distortion are always the same – a straightforward statement of the time to be distorted. For instance: 'In just one minute of clock time, you will experience thirty minutes of subjective time'; or, alternatively, the state-ment can be left ambiguous, but with specified limits, e.g. 'you will, in one minute of clock time, solve this problem which normally takes about thirty minutes'. Both of these are examples of time expansion, which have a number of non-medical uses, as we shall see in later chapters. Time contraction is more difficult, but why this is so is not known. It has many uses in clinical situations, most notably, shortening the time a pain is experienced. In the next section, we shall illustrate the use of time contraction in shortening the subjective experience of the time that a journey takes.

### Time expansion 1: The Time Machine
In this session, [name], you are going to expand time. One

minute of clock time is going to feel like thirty minutes to you. Yes, [name], in one minute, you are going to feel as if thirty minutes have elapsed, and this time distortion will remain until I normalize it once again.

[Name], you are sitting in a time machine, just like the one created in H. G. Wells' novel by that name, and you are seated before a window, through which you have no difficulty in seeing out. You now push the lever forward and time begins to speed up. You can see things moving across the window, and they are moving faster and faster, yes they are moving faster and faster. Day becomes night, and then night becomes day. And the night follows the day, more and more quickly. The seasons now become noticeable, because time is moving very, very quickly. And now it all goes dark. (pause)

Your time is now slowing down to normal. Yes, [name], your sense of time has returned to normal. With no difficulty at all, you are now back to normal.

During this set of suggestions, a variety of sensations will probably be experienced. The most conspicuous is a sense of speed. Furthermore, the whole suggestion will probably take a few minutes of clock time, but your subjective experience of the lapse of time will be much longer. Although you suggested one minute into thirty this is unlikely to be the actual distortion, although the difference will become longer with practice. During this sequence, you may also dissociate, as you may in other time distortion experiments.

A variant of the above, which will appeal to the scientist or science fiction lover, is the following. In this, we will not again repeat the distortion, and we shall shorten the instructions because they are basically the same as for the time machine. You can elaborate, and above all, picture the whole sequence.

### Time expansion 2: Space Travel

(Stipulate the time distortion first, then continue.) You are on a disc, tied down securely. The disc is below a dome on the roof which opens up to the sky. And now the disc begins to spin, faster and faster (repeat, increasing the speed).

The dome now opens and you fly out off into space. You pass the planets, the stars, etc., going faster and faster. And you are

now being pulled into a black hole, ever faster (repeat). You are now through the black hole where time is motionless and everything is dark and peaceful.
[Now return your sense of time to normality.]

This set of instructions will, in all probability, elicit the same sensations as the first, with the possible exception of the final stage, which can produce a blackness and feeling of emptiness far greater than you may have experienced before. This particular instruction may also cause a far greater degree of dissociation. In addition, both instructions will deepen the hypnotic state automatically, because of the deep involvement in the subjective experiences.

Time contraction is more difficult to elicit and it is generally more difficult to devise scenes that will help in developing this technique. The object, however, is for you to create a scene in which you become very involved and that would generally take a long time for such an event or situation to unfold. In this way a long journey, for instance, can be passed without too much notice: a two or three hour journey can be reduced to thirty minutes or so. The more involved and detailed the scene, the longer your attention will be held by this and not focused on the journey.

### Time Contraction
Thirty minutes of actual time are going to feel like five minutes to you. Yes, [name], time is going to go by very very quickly, just as it does whenever you become very interested in something. Yes, in thirty minutes of subjective time, your entire journey of three hours is going to be over.
[Now create the most vivid scene you can, paying attention to details, no matter how small. Be involved in it. More importantly, have a clock somewhere in the scene which strikes twelve, and between each strike continue to elaborate on the scene. A fairy tale or something from the Arabian Nights is ideal.]

The object, of course, is to become involved in the scene. To become so interested and involved that your attention becomes very directed to it. This slows down your subjective sense of time and so actual time goes more quickly.

## Uses of Time Distortion

It is apparent that time distortion refers only to mental thinking, and not to physical responses of the body. Even with time expansion, you cannot build a doll's house in half the time. You can, however, reduce the objective time taken from the amount of time you would normally take. But we shall return to this later. The point being made at the moment is that the uses of time distortion are limited to mental actions. Under hypnosis and using time expansion, it is possible in five clock minutes or so to re-experience the reading of a whole novel or to see, once again, the whole of *Gone with the Wind*. As explained earlier, this is likely to arise from the holographic nature of the mind.

The suggestion used to elicit experiences of this nature, is as follows:

> **Re-experiencing a Whole Film or Novel in Five Minutes**
> In a moment, when I say, you will imagine that you are once again watching *Gone With the Wind*, and only five minutes of clock time will be required for you to watch, once again, the whole of the film, with no difficulty at all, and in all its detail. Now imagine you are seeing the film.

There is more to this than watching a film. The brain records all past and present experiences. Under hypnosis, these can be recalled much easier than normal and, certainly, in more detail than normal. Combined with time expansion, you can re-read a whole book, for instance, and so help your memory and recall. As an educational device, this is extremely valuable – and it costs nothing! In Chapter 11, these educational applications of self-hypnosis will be discussed further.

Here, I wish to consider further just one other non-medical use of time distortion: namely, solving a problem. Solving problems, whether they are to do with the household or are of a more technical nature, are both time-consuming and require the expenditure of a great deal of energy. This loss of energy often goes unnoticed, except when the problem is solved. Then, a sense of relief is usually felt, which is quite noticeable. Alternatively, those people who worry about problems at the unconscious level, tend to create tensions somewhere in the musculature of their bodies – especially in the walls of the stomach (which also tend to aggravate ulcers).

The act of hypnosis reduces tensions, and allows you to approach a given problem more effectively and more object-ively. By also using time distortion, you can amass in your mind all the relevant facts, and begin to solve the problem in far less time than you would take in your normal waking state. The reason for this should now be fairly apparent. Under hypnosis, you are concerned only about that which you have decided to direct your attention to, namely the problem, at the exclusion of everything else. Second, you have reduced your general level of tension, which allows more energy to be directed at the problem – rather than in a wasteful tension of the muscles. Third, your recall of information is far superior to normal. Finally, by speeding up the process, you can obtain a better understanding of the different facets of the problem, which, in turn, helps in formulating a solution more quickly – and almost certainly a better solution, if more than one exists.

Let me expand on this issue a little longer. Suppose you cannot keep all the facts, etc., in your head, or that you wish to write out steps in obtaining the solution, or to draw a diagram. In other words, suppose that, in coming to a solution, you must consider material that you have gathered, constructed, sketched, or whatever. In this case, you wish to approach the solution somewhat differently. The first job is to hypnotize yourself and then carry out a time distortion instruction. Having done this, you then give yourself the following suggestions:

### Problem-solving
In a moment, when I say, you will open your eyes and you will go to your desk (table, or whatever), which has all the necessary information that you require in considering your problem. And because five minutes of clock time are going to feel like thirty minutes to you, then you will find that the solution to the problem will arise quicker than normal. You will be able to marshall all the facts very easily, and the solution will come to you very easily and very quickly.
Now open your eyes and go to work.

If necessary, elaborate the suggestions with specific details, in the light of whatever problem you are trying to solve.

It is also possible to use this technique in earlier stages, such as setting out the problem, seeing whether the problem can be looked at in a variety of ways. Creativity is a right brain feature and, under hypnosis, this has a greater chance of arising. If your work involves design, then, at this stage, engage in self-hypnosis so that you can apply the creativity which we all possess, but under-utilize.

The educational value of time distortion is very great and is quite underrated in the literature on hypnosis, largely, I feel, because of the greater emphasis on the medical uses of hypnosis. This is the cost of allowing the medical profession to monopolize the training of professional hypnotists.

## Time Distortion and Post-Hypnotic Suggestions

In the previous section, I highlighted the use of time expansion as an aid in solving problems. Another possibility is to combine time distortion with a post-hypnotic suggestion. We shall do this with the use of time contraction, since we have not used this feature as frequently as time expansion.

Chores of one sort and another are, to many people, a drudgery, and because they are such a drudgery, they seem to take a long time to do, either as measured by the clock and/or in terms of subjective time. Just as we do not like waiting for a bus and, as a consequence, it seems to take ages in coming, so with unpleasant tasks such as housework. It is true that some people like housework, but for many it is something which must be tolerated, no matter how distasteful. In this section, I shall concentrate on this one example as an illustration of the use of time contraction with a post-hypnotic suggestion. It can be readily adapted to other situations.

I shall first give the instructions and then discuss them, referring to the numbers in brackets. First induce hypnosis. There is no need to carry out a time distortion because this will be contained in the post-hypnotic suggestion.

Housework (or any disagreeable job)
[Name], when you awaken, you will go about doing your housework. You will begin with the living room, then on to the

kitchen, etc. (1). Visualize this now. See yourself, going through each room, doing all that is necessary. (2)

And while you are doing this, which you will do when you awaken, time is going to go very slowly indeed. You will be able to get through all of your housework in no time at all. You will concentrate on each task and think of nothing else. (repeat) (3).

You will feel happy and will direct all your attention to the task in hand. Yes, you will go from the living room to the kitchen, and then on to ...

And time is going to go very slowly and before you know it, in no time at all, the housework will be done and you will be very pleased and most satisfied with your progress and what you have accomplished.

Let me now explain the three points. (1) It is useful to have a clear idea of which rooms and in what order you wish to do the housework, and to do this *before* you induce hypnosis. This is so that you can give yourself the instructions without having to think about it, for to think about it will activate your left brain. The order is purely illustrative, but it is best to begin with the most disagreeable task because the post-hypnotic suggestion will be strongest at this stage. This approach also has the advantage that, as the jobs get shorter, you will, quite naturally, take less time to do them, and so the success of the suggestions will act as a reinforcement.

(2) It is very important to carry out the visualization. Actually see yourself hoovering the floor, washing the dishes, etc. Furthermore, see yourself doing these in a very happy frame of mind – singing if you like that. In all likelihood, you will do the work very much as pictured. If you can, try introducing some fun into the whole affair. A job is not, in itself, a drudgery: it is your attitude towards the job that makes it so. Knowing this, it can be eliminated and even replaced by something else. So why not introduce some humour into the whole affair. If you have children, include them in the work and turn it into a game. Be imaginative, and housework, or any job, can take on a totally new dimension.

(3) This is an important suggestion. It can be referred to as the principle of one-pointed attention. Jobs often take longer than necessary because a person's whole attention is not on the

job in hand. How often are we doing one thing while thinking about something else? This should be avoided at all costs. This one-pointed attention should be cultivated in all things you do, and not just in this post-hypnotic suggestion concerning housework. The more busy you are, especially if this means you have a variety of jobs to deal with, then the more important it is to deal with each problem in turn, and devote all your attention to that one task. When this is done, then and only then should you turn your attention to the next job. If you do have many jobs, always work out in advance of the hypnotic induction, the sequence in which they are to be carried out. I shall return to one-pointed attention in Chapter 11, where a specific set of instructions for achieving it will be given.

# 9
# INCREASING YOUR SELF-CONFIDENCE

In this chapter, I shall be concerned with the issue of self-confidence, in particular, the lack of self-confidence. One commonly hears that Joe Bloggs is 'full of self-confidence', or that he 'lacks self-confidence'. Such everyday statements should not blind us to the fact that self-confidence is not an attribute which a person has or does not have. It is a matter of degree. A person is confident when he feels comfortable in his immediate environment, and feels comfortable that he can cope with any change that is likely in such an environment. This particular formulation of self-confidence has two important features which are worth stressing. First, the less familiar you are with your immediate environment, or the less familiar you are with the likely changes in that environment, then the more you are likely to exhibit signs of anxiety which, in turn, may lead to a reduction in your feeling of self-confidence. Of course, anxiety can arise from many causes, but the association with reduced self-confidence arises from the relationship you have with your immediate environment.

Take a simple example. A man or woman appears to their friends very self-confident, at least at work and at home. Now the man goes abroad. The immediate environment is strange and the person is unsure how to act. This leads, initially at least, to some anxiety and a reduction in his usual degree of self-confidence. The more frequently he goes abroad, the more familiar he becomes with the new environment and the likely changes in that environment, and so the more sure he becomes: his usual self-confidence begins to return, as his anxiety diminishes.

This example also illustrates the second feature of this formulation of self-confidence, which is that reduced self-confidence is attached to certain situations – except in extreme cases. We can be self-confident in one situation, but lack it in another. The reason, as the example illustrates, is that one situation occurs in a familiar environment, whilst the other does not. How we respond to new or changing environments is a behaviour pattern which is acquired over a lifetime.

The situation, just outlined, is very important to understand, because it hints at how you may overcome mild forms of reduced self-confidence. The first job, however, is to take a mental note of the situations where your self-confidence is lacking most, and, especially, take note of the environment in which it occurs. Second, rather than avoid such situations, which is the fairly common reaction, go out of your way to encounter them frequently. By so doing, the unfamiliar becomes the familiar and anxiety is accordingly reduced. This can, of course, be undertaken without the use of self-hypnosis; but, as stated repeatedly in this book, by using hypnosis, the change in behaviour can be accomplished quicker and, certainly, more effectively.

It must be stressed that this chapter will be concerned with forms of reduced self-confidence, most particularly those that arise in unfamiliar circumstances. If you have to do some one-off event then, by definition, you will not have had any past experience of exactly this kind. The degree of anxiety you feel, will depend on how many similar situations you have undertaken, and the degree of similarity. Hypnosis can relieve the anxiety and can, by means of images, bring the familiarity which in such circumstances is not available. You can become familiar with the situation in your mind's eye, and so raise your self-confidence at the moment you undertake whatever it is you have agreed to do.

Any general high degree of reduced self-confidence or a

high general level of anxiety should be dealt with by a specialist. When hypnosis is used in such a treatment, it is referred to as hypnotherapy. Such analysis should not be done by yourself, unless under the guidance of a specialist. This chapter is *not* concerned with such extreme cases.

## Positive Thinking

Norman Vincent Peale in his famous book, *The Power of Positive Thinking*, demonstrates that lack of self-confidence can arise from negative thinking, while self-confidence can arise from positive thinking. More important is the feature of reinforcement. Involved in reinforcement is both a quantitative and a qualitative aspect. Something is reinforced if you repeat it a sufficient number of times – a feature most important to the success of hypnosis in general. Repetition, however, must be accompanied by belief. It is possible for you to repeat a positive statement twenty times, but if you do not believe it, then just one negative statement in which you do believe can wipe away the twenty!

Fortunately, repetition and belief are not independent of one another. If something is repeated often enough, then it will eventually be believed. The object of positive thinking is to fill your thoughts with only positive statements, which, if repeated, will be self reinforcing. The more you can believe in them, the more effective they will be. Just as, when you look for the bad, you are sure to find it, so when you look for the good then this, with practice, will also be found.

We can combine positive thinking with the idea that reduced self-confidence arises from new situations that must be faced. We must always approach a new or changing environment with a positive attitude. By doing this, anxiety is reduced. Why? A negative approach highlights the uniqueness of the situation, and the fact that you have never dealt with this before. A positive attitude instills the idea that you have dealt with a number of similar situations in your life before and, on each occasion, there was something in the situation that was new and rewarding for you.

The mental attitude with which you approach a situation is of vital importance. You should, at all times, see the bright side and take a positive approach. If you find this difficult, then use self-hypnosis to bring about a positive approach to life. Try something like the following:

### Positive Approach to Thinking

[Name], from now on, you are going to take a positive approach to everything. You are going to eliminate all negative thoughts from your thinking, and you are going to replace them with positive ones. Each time you have a negative thought, you will immediately replace it by a positive one; and, over time, you will discover that you will have less and less negative thoughts. And you will also find that having constantly positive thoughts will make you more cheerful and much less anxious. You will strive to think only positively and you will find that, in the future, this will become easier and easier to do.

Notice, in this instruction, the post-hypnotic nature of the suggestions; the fact that the response will occur in the future and that changes will be noticed as the actions are carried out. It is important to repeat this at regular intervals, so that the suggestions are reinforced, thus assuring their success. The whole process is one of counter-conditioning. You are trying to create a change in your behaviour, which has arisen over many years. So do not expect the suggestions to create a change overnight.

As they are presented, no imagery is incorporated, but it is useful to do so. You could include, or just imagine, a situation where a negative thought is wiped out with a cloth, deleted in some way or other. Let P stand for positive statements and N for negative and imagine the Ns being wiped out. Let a string of Ps and Ns represent your thoughts over the coming months and see the Ns getting less and less until only Ps can be seen. Not only see this, but believe it.

Any suggestions that create an attitude of positive thinking will also have the effect of raising your self-confidence.

### Suggestions for Increasing Self-Confidence

This section falls into two parts. First, suggestions for some specific occasion and secondly, a set of instructions for a general raising of self-confidence.

There are a variety of situations we encounter which are

either unique or unfamiliar, and so may lead to anxiety. Such anxiety makes us self-conscious and has the effect of reducing our performance below our full potential. It may be that we have to meet someone for the first time and wish to make an impression; it may be that we have to give a talk to a group of strangers; it may be simply joining a large group where everyone will be a stranger to you. The situation I wish to deal with, however, is the job interview. This always has the feature of being unique and no matter how many interviews a person goes through they will always be anxious, to some degree, on such occasions. Of course, the idea can readily be applied to any event where you wish to give yourself some support and bolster up your self-confidence.

The suggestions have two basic objectives. First, they aim to reduce negative thoughts and replace them with positive ones. Second, they are used to carry out an imaginary interview, in which you perform exceptionally well and, of course, become appointed.

Before we begin, however, it is important to note that the instructions here, and in the more general case given later, direct your attention to three aspects:

  (i)   Thinking
 (ii)   Feeling
(iii)   Behaviour

It is important that all these are covered in the suggestions, so that they can reinforce each other. Although, on occasions, all three are involved simultaneously, this is not always the case. Furthermore, the lack of self-confidence may manifest itself in one or other of these three aspects more strongly and hence, more attention must be given to this. Take the case of the person who is 'all talk and no action'. Such a person may have positive thinking and may have the right feelings, but, unconsciously, cannot put these into action. In this situation, therefore, more attention must be directed at putting thoughts and feelings into action.

Right, then, you have agreed to attend an interview in the near future. It may be useful to make up a tape which you can play until the time of the interview and then wipe clean. The time taken will more than pay dividends. Your instructions may go something like this:

### Interview

[Name], shortly, you will be going for an interview for ... This is a job that you particularly want and so it is important for you to make a good impression at your interview (pause). You have a suitable background and any deficiencies can be made up once the job is underway, so that there is no difficulty there. Anyway, you cannot, in the time, correct any deficiencies and so there is no point concerning yourself with this. In addition, it is difficult to know what is required without having sampled the job (pause). So you will attend, on the assumption that your background is as good, if not better, than other candidates (pause).

Now, [name], picture yourself going to the interview. See yourself calm and collected, having had a good night's sleep the evening before, and you are feeling fresh and bright. Also see yourself cheerful and, above all, see yourself confident. You can now see yourself waiting and yet not feeling nervous. It is often the waiting which is worst, but you will find that this is going to pass very quickly indeed. Yes, no matter how long your waiting is by clock time, you will *feel* the time simply rushing by and, in no time at all, it will be your turn to be interviewed (pause).

And now you go into the room, yes, you can picture it all very clearly. You are sitting in the chair, facing the interviewing panel. And they begin to ask you questions, and these questions you answer easily and confidently. Even awkward questions are dealt with and, at all times, you are feeling confident, but not over-confident (pause). Your confidence shows, both in the content of your replies and how well you reply. Nobody likes to employ someone who is not sure of themselves. And so you are going to be sure and confident (pause).

You will have questions for them and, in preparation for these, you will find out something about the firm, the industry, the location, etc. You will show an interest in the job you have applied for and in the company (pause).

And, at all times, you will feel calm, relaxed and confident. You will, throughout the interview, believe absolutely that you will be offered the job, you will believe in yourself and that you are capable of doing the job (pause).

And you will now see yourself coming out of the interview, feeling delighted and satisfied with the whole affair. And, throughout, you will feel relaxed and confident, just as you will be relaxed and confident on the day (pause). The day will go just as you have seen it go just now. Nothing is going to upset you, and you are going to be calm, relaxed and confident throughout.

We now turn to a method of increasing self-confidence that will apply generally. In this set of instructions we shall make use of voice intonation. Where such words are to be stressed, we shall set these in italics. These are most important, as are the pauses which are indicated throughout. This is a fairly lengthy set of instructions, but even so, they should, if put on a cassette tape, be capable of being contained on one side only. The first part of the tape should include an induction and deepening so that the whole set of instructions can be done in one sitting. Throughout, you should try to visualize yourself in all the types of situations that are referred to. After the induction and deepening, try the following routine, taken from *Medical and Dental Hypnosis and Its Clinical Applications* by J. Hartland (Balliere Tindall, 1971), which is a particularly useful set of suggestions because it also highlights the importance of voice intonation, which are highlighted in italics:

### General Increased Self-Confidence
You are now so deeply relaxed that your mind is *extremely* sensitive and receptive to what I am saying and *everything* that I say to you now will sink *so* deeply into your unconscious mind that it will cause a deep and lasting impression there, *so* deep and lasting that *nothing* will be able to eradicate it from your unconscious mind (pause). Consequently, these suggestions which I am now giving you are going deep into your unconscious mind, and they will begin to exercise a greater and greater influence over the way you think, over the way you feel and over the way you behave (pause). And these things *will* happen, and *will* remain firmly embedded in the unconscious part of your mind, *so* that from the time you awaken

they will continue to exercise that same influence – over your *thoughts* and over your *feelings* and over your *actions* (pause). This influence will be *just* as *strong* and *just* as *powerful* when you awaken as they are now. Yes, every feeling that you will experience when I tell you, you *will* experience it exactly as I tell you. And these experiences will continue to be felt every day; yes, and you will continue to experience these feelings each and every day (pause). And you will continue to experience them every day *just* as *strongly* and *just* as *powerfully* as you do now (pause).

During this session, now in fact, you are going to feel physically fit, physically strong and better in every way. And besides feeling more fit, you are also *now* feeling more alert. Yes, although your eyes are closed, you are *more* alert, *more* wide awake, and *more* energetic than you have ever been before. And you will become less easily tired, *much* less easily fatigued, and *much* less easily discouraged or depressed (pause).

Every day you will become *so deeply interested* in whatever you are doing and whatever is going on around you, that your mind *will* become very distracted away from yourself. You will *no longer* think nearly so much about yourself, about your difficulties, and you *will* become *less* conscious of yourself, much less preoccupied with yourself and with your own feelings (pause).

Each day, your nerves *will* become stronger and steadier, and you *will* become calmer and *more* composed and *more* tranquil with each day that passes. Yes, with each day that passes, you will become *much less* worried and *much less* agitated, *much less* fearful and *much less* apprehensive, so that you will become *much less* upset (pause). You *will* be able to think more clearly and you *will* be able to concentrate more easily on whatever you are doing. Yes, you *will* give your whole undivided attention to whatever you are doing, and you will do this to the complete exclusion of everything else (pause). As a consequence, you will be able to see things more clearly and in their true perspective, so that difficulties will not become magnified. Yes, you will have perspective and not let things get out of proportion (pause).

Every day, you will become emotionally *much* calmer and *much more* settled and *much less* easily disturbed. Every day you *will* become *more* relaxed, and every day you *will* become *less* tense, yes, less physically tense and less mentally tense (pause).

And, as you become *more* relaxed and *less* tense each day, so you will remain more relaxed and less tense, you will develop *much more* confidence in yourself, *more* confidence in your ability to do things. *More* confidence in your ability to do each day those things that have to be done, *more* confidence to do each day those things that ought to be done (pause). And you *will* be *so* confident in your ability that you will have *no* fear of failure, you will have *no* fear of the consequences because you will be confident that these will turn out right, and you will have no unnecessary anxiety or uneasiness in doing what has to be done and what ought to be done (pause).

Because of this, each day you will feel *more and more* independent, yes, more and more independent, so that you are *more able* to stand up for yourself and to stand on your own two feet. Yes, you will become more confident, *so* that you can hold your own, no matter how difficult or trying things may appear to be (pause).

Each day will bring with it a *greater* feeling of well-being and safety. Yes, situations will no longer create fear or anxiety. And because of this, you *will* feel more secure and *much more* confident (pause).

You will depend more and more on your own judgement and on your own decisions, and you will be able to express your own opinions with confidence. You will listen to others, but you will not depend on them (pause).

Yes, all these things will begin to happen. And *just* as they are happening now in your mind's eye, *so* they are going to happen to you in the future. As each day passes, *so* these suggestions will become *more* powerful and *so* you will begin to feel *more and more* confident (pause). *More and more* happy, *more* content and *more* optimistic in every way (pause).

Although you may not notice these changes immediately, you *do* know that these suggestions are going deep down into your unconscious mind, and *so* as you repeat these suggestions as frequently as you can, they will begin to have a *more and more* powerful influence on you as each day passes.

Although this has been a long instruction, it is a most important one. It has the general characteristics of boosting your self-confidence. More significant, is the fact that it involves repeated post-hypnotic suggestions. If these instructions are taped and the tape is played frequently enough, then the effects (responses) will undoubtedly occur, and your future will become a happier and a more secure one. Do not, however, expect immediate changes.

Persistent use of these instructions will sow the seed for a more fundamental and secure change in your mental attitude – a change that you yourself have decided on and will have brought about.

# 10
# SELF-HYPNOSIS AND SPORT

There has recently been considerable interest shown in the relationship between imagery and sport, under the general title of 'inner games', made most popular by T. Gallaway in *The Inner Game of Tennis*, and followed, (in collaboration with B. Kriegal) with *Inner Skiing*. There is, however, nothing new about this process, what *is* new is the demonstration of the wide scope and power that imagination has. To a large extent, the 'inner game revolution' is a sign that the earlier idea, that the mind and body are totally independent, is simply not true. Yogis have argued this for many years, but it was not until intensive research had been carried out on such people, that Western science would admit that the autonomic nervous system can be influenced by the mind.

Most of this book has been demonstrating just this fact. The basic argument being put forward in this book is that the autonomic nervous system, because it is automatic, is a right brain function. This does not mean that it cannot be brought under conscious control; on the contrary, it can. The problem is that it cannot be achieved through logic or reason. In other words, left brain features are not sufficient to carry out this task. It has repeatedly been stated in this book that Western man has been left brain dominated. There has been a tendency to argue that what cannot be consciously perceived –

and by this we should read it to be, what cannot be conceived by the left brain – cannot exist. This narrow view of the mind has limited Western man and, most particularly, has meant he has not attained anything like his full potential.

Sport is about movement, rhythm, co-ordination, and synchronization – all of which are features of the right brain. The intention of this chapter is to illustrate how self-hypnosis can be used in *all* sports, and not simply in tennis. You need not be an Olympic champion who is attempting to better his style or form. No, you can simply be someone who wishes to improve his game, whichever game that happens to be.

We play sport for the purpose of toning up our bodies and for the pleasure it brings. This second feature is most revealing. We have argued that the right brain operates according to the pleasure principle, and we have a fitting demonstration of this in sport. The pleasure takes place while you are playing, and although it continues after the game is over, it is an immediate experience. You cannot separate the game from the enjoyment. We learn something until our movements become spontaneous and automatic. When we try to consciously think about what we are doing, we usually make things worse: we become self-conscious. In other words, instead of using just the right brain, we bring into operation the left brain too. But the left brain is not suited for this function. The surgeon does not begin his operation with a kitchen knife, rather he uses his scalpel, because this has been specifically designed for this purpose. So why should we be any different? Why should we not use the hemisphere of the brain that was specifically designed for certain tasks when we undertake such tasks?

In the first section, I shall discuss some illustrative examples from sport, in which the importance of mental attitude has already been recognized for some time. In so doing, these attitudes will be related to our previous analysis. In particular, I shall emphasize how sportsmen and sportswomen establish a 'mental set'. In the following section, some specific suggestions for generally improving sport will be given. This will be broken down into (a) training, (b) performance, and (c) 'on the day'. I shall then deal with issues which more directly concern amateur and professional sportspeople; namely, how to deal with periods of illness and injury; and second, how to deal with loss of confidence. In the final section, I shall make some general observations about the use of self-hypnosis in sport.

### The 'Mental Set' in Sport

It is well known that a number of sportspeople 'psyche themselves up' before a game. This takes a variety of forms, depending on the sport, but the purpose, in each case, is the same. It is to establish a 'mental set' which is most conducive to creating the right atmosphere. Billie Jean King is known to have done this before her tennis matches, and weight-lifters do it before each lift. In fact, with weight-lifters, you can actually see it in operation, even though it is a brief procedure. A number of sportspeople go through some form of routine, some ritual, prior to a game. This is also establishing a 'mental set'. Ritual is, by no means, a case of following blindly something you are supposed to do because, historically, that is the way it is done. Ritual has the important function of creating a 'mental set' and activating the right brain.

The importance of a 'mental set' and, in particular, the influence of the mind on the body, has been influenced by the existence of *psychological limits* in a number of sports. For a long time, four minutes remained a psychological lower limit for fast runners of the mile. It was believed that this could not be done, until accomplished by Roger Bannister. A more revealing psychological upper limit was that of 500lb in weight-lifting. Again, it was believed that this could not be exceeded. It was broken by Valery Alexis by being 'fooled' into believing he was lifting less than 500lb when, in fact, it was just over this weight. The importance of these illustrations is the fact that belief plays a role in performance, along with training. Without training (and possibly even with training), most of us could not run a four-minute mile or lift 500lb of weight – even if belief is strong. With training *and* belief, then more things are possible. Why? Because both the right and the left brains are contributing to performance, and contributing those aspects for which they are designed.

Each sport is likely to have its own best 'mental set', but so little attention has been given to this aspect that these have not been established. Individuals are expected to find their own by trial and error, or hope that their coach can give them a suitable one. Short of establishing a 'mental set', let us examine how you can use imagery and self-hypnosis to improve your game.

## Improving Your Sport

We can approach this more practical section from three aspects. First, how to improve your period of training. Second, how to improve your actual performance in any particular pursuit you are undertaking. Third, how to improve your performance on the day you actually perform. We have separated these three aspects, so that the type of suggestions for each, can be clearly distinguished.

Training is required in any sport if you wish to progress. This is stating the obvious, but it is based on the idea that training allows certain actions to become automatic and, by becoming automatic, they are carried out by the right brain. In the process of training, you concentrate on the task in hand, which means that you direct your attention to this task and this task alone. To improve training, therefore, we need to improve concentration. Second, training is required to establish a fair degree of co-ordination between our body parts, and our mind in relation to our body, in order to achieve an unconstrained performance – whether in swinging a racquet at a tennis ball or in skating.

Your training should be approached with the same ritual as would be performed on the actual occasion you play or participate, so as to establish a 'mental set' with which you become familiar. The more direct use of self-hypnosis is a relaxation and suggestion session just prior to your training. The aim of this is to mentally go through your training in your mind's eye and carry out appropriate post-hypnotic suggestions. To make the suggestions a little more concrete, we shall suppose your training consists of no more than a variety of gym exercises. Although not directed at any specific sport, this will give sufficient indication of what is to be done, so that you can adapt it to your own specific needs.

Throughout these suggestions, you should see yourself in the gym, actually carrying out all the exercises. This image should be as vivid as possible. A typical set of training suggestions may take the following form. First hypnotize yourself, deepen and attain a deep relaxed state and then continue as follows:

Training Suggestions
In a moment, you will be going into the gym to train. On this occasion, your training is going to consist of general exercises (or whatever). You are going to approach the training with enthusiasm and expectation, the expectation that this training is going to make your body supple, strong and fitter to carry out [state some specific sport].
Yes, you are going to train very well. You are going to concentrate solely on the training and nothing else. All the time, you are going to know and feel that the training is going to make you better in every way.
You can see yourself at this moment training. You can see yourself lifting weights (pause), stepping on and off the bench (pause) ....
[Simply go through *all* of what you do in training. See yourself actually doing the exercises – to the best of your ability.]
And, [name], you are not going to become tired or fatigued. You will find that you have more energy than you ever had before. Your training is going to be a most pleasant experience and a very fulfilling one.
[Name], you will know instinctively where you have been failing in the past and know what it is you must practise most. And the whole session is going to be most enjoyable and satisfying.

If you are training for something specific, simply incorporate this into the suggestions. What is important in the above suggestions, is that they raise your expectancy, and involve repeated post-hypnotic suggestions concerning the time you actually undertake your training in the gym. As I have repeated, use your imagination and picture the whole scene as vividly as you can.
One point is worth commenting on at this stage. The suggestions include the phrase: 'You are not going to become tired or fatigued'. Does this mean that you may over-exert yourself by such a post-hypnotic suggestion? The simple

answer is 'No'. Your muscles and your body in general have their own built-in safety device with a variety of signals to warn you. The suggestion merely acts on your will, on your motivation during the training, and ensures that it remains positive – that your left and right brains are working to achieve the same end. That is all. The suggestion can allow you to stretch yourself – to achieve your full potential – it cannot possibly give you the ability to go beyond it. That is the point of training, to extend your physical abilities and so your potential.

Let me now turn to performance. It will help, in illustrating this, to consider a specific example. Suppose we take the high jump. The object of this exercise is two fold. First, to visualize the actual event, and secondly, to exaggerate 'beyond the reasonable'. Why carry out this second aspect? To visualize the actual event and actual performance is very useful, and certainly utilizes your right brain functions. You are not, however, using *all* of your right brain functions. It is like a runner who trains his muscles, but ignores his breathing! Obviously, he can perform well if he trains his muscles, but the point is that he can perform better still if he trains both his muscles *and* his breathing. But why the exaggeration? We come back to the idea that the right brain does not work on logic or reason; it works by means of pictures and symbols. The meaning of these become much clearer, the more bizarre and exaggerated the picture. It is this aspect which, unfortunately, is missing from the 'inner games' as normally outlined.

The basic point about this suggestion under self-hypnosis, is that it can be done in the quiet of your own home, without any apparatus and in all kinds of weather! So let us illustrate, by means of the high jump. You can of course replace it with anything you like.

### Improving Your Performance

Tomorrow, [or whenever], you are going to be carrying out the high jump. But now, simply see yourself performing it. You are making ready, you can visualize yourself running up and you can see yourself carrying out a perfect jump.

And now the bar is being raised and, once again, you carry out a perfect jump. And you are pleased with your performance.

You are relaxed and it just seems to come very naturally.

Now the bar is placed at the highest position you have jumped so far. You can see yourself preparing to jump this again. And because you have done it before, you are confident that you can do it on this occasion: with ease, as if you have done this height very frequently in your training. And you run up, you can see yourself clearing the bar with ease and, more importantly, with plenty of room to spare. So much room, in fact, that if the bar was raised, you would have no difficulty in clearing that height also.

And the bar is raised. But this does not worry you at all. You know that you can clear it because before you had so much clearance. And now you see yourself running and jumping, and you clear the bar with ease, with no difficulty at all.

[You may continue with one or two more notches. But then change the suggestion totally.]

You are now on the moon or some distant planet where the gravity is very low and, normally, people wear leaded boots. And today, on this planet, there is a series of games, in which you are performing the high jump. But this is not like on earth. The jumps are miles high, and the height is not a bar, but a mountain which you have to leap over.

And you see yourself do this with ease. And you can feel the extreme lightness which allows you to almost fly over the mountain. And it is a most exhilarating feeling.

And to your surprise, you find that when you return to earth, you retain some of this lightness, this feeling that you could simply fly through the air and that the normal height of the bar is no obstacle whatsoever.

And tomorrow, this same feeling will occur and you will be able to jump higher than you have done in the past.

I should think by now you get the idea. Notice, in particular, that in the latter part of the suggestion, the idea that the same feeling *will continue* when you return to earth is a very important post-hypnotic suggestion. Also notice that throughout the instructions, there are suggestions of confidence and ease.

Suggestions for dealing with the day and event concerned, need not be given in detail, because they are very similar to those just given for improving your performance. The major difference is in creating a clear visual picture of the actual event, including the actual surroundings, as you can. Furthermore, you should include suggestions of confidence, that the performance of other participants will in no way undermine the confidence you have in your own ability. Most important is that you must generate a *feeling* of confidence and success. Stating confidence and success is a left brain function, *feeling* confident and successful is a right brain attribute. So you must believe it and feel it. The visualization can aid this. Make sure that, having succeeded, you see and feel the elation of having done so. See people congratulating you and see how pleased you are and feel the pleasure *now*.

## Injury and Loss of Confidence

To the average person, an injury simply means that a sport is dispensed with for a while. For an amateur and professional, however, it can be a major blow to their future prospects. The same basically applies to a loss of confidence, which is why we are treating them together in the one section. But let me take each one in turn.

Let us suppose you are a budding Robin Cousins and that you sustain an injury that involves you staying in bed for a certain period. Rather than feeling sorry for yourself, this can be a good opportunity to practise self-hypnosis, and to use the self-hypnosis to carry out practice sessions and training.

We need not go into this in detail, because the basic idea is to carry out the type of suggestions indicated in the previous section. You should carry out training sessions and performances in your mind's eye, fairly frequently, at least once a day. If you are laid up in bed, this can be an alternative to reading or watching TV. During this period, it is a good idea to find some particularly bizarre scene that you can conjure up, which will both occupy your time and allow you to perform an inner game. Create a fairytale – don't be bashful! Imagine that some wicked wizard has done something to you that turned you into something, which means that you cannot skate. Then some handsome prince (or beautiful princess) releases you from the curse and you skate together in some wondrous place, feeling as if your whole being was part of the movement, as if you were made just to skate. Just be imaginative. Each day, or every few days, create a new scene until you find this easy to do. Certainly it will be more enjoyable than simply lying there in bed.

When you do your training or performances during a hypnotic session like this, make sure that you picture everything in detail. Furthermore, feel yourself performing each act. Of course, always picture a success – never a failure. Go over each routine in the minutest detail until it becomes part of you. From what has been said in this book, it should be clear that the object of the inner game is to make it become part of your unconscious mind, to make the movements instinctive. Visual imagery can be just as powerful, and on some occasions more powerful, at accomplishing this than training alone.

Do not turn your injury into defeat, turn it into even greater success. Give yourself post-hypnotic suggestions that you are going to return, not only fit and healthy, but with a far superior style and ability than you had before your injury.

Loss of confidence is less straightforward because it depends on why it occurred. But take a page out of Mohammed Ali's book. He exuded confidence, so much so that he often demoralized his opponents. Loss of confidence is purely psychological and, as such, can be eliminated by means of suggestion. Follow the basic theme of Chapter 9, but direct the suggestion towards your attitude to the sport. Convince yourself that such a lack of confidence is purely a negative suggestion which can be eliminated and replaced by self-confidence and positive suggestions. Repeat this frequently and, above all, take a positive attitude.

## Some Final Observations
Research carried out on hypnotic subjects indicates that those involved in group sports, such as football, are likely to be more hypnotizable than those involved in individual sports. We have already explained the reason for this *statistical* tendency. It rests on the fact that people involved in group sports must take instructions from the coach or captain, and must be willing to do so. On this basis, they have had more practice at cultivating those attributes which enable a person to enter a hypnotic state. At the same time, it should not have gone

unnoticed that all the examples used, so far, in this chapter are individual sports.

Two basic questions arise from these observations. First, can a person who belongs to a team engage in 'inner games'? Second, do the remarks in this chapter indicate that there is more potential for betterment by persons who compete largely on an individual basis? The quick answer to both questions is, yes.

Take the case of a footballer who is injured and wishes to use self-hypnosis while he is laid up in bed. The basic idea is to utilize the suggestions very much on the lines given in the previous section, the major difference being that you must visualize all the players, (or those in your vicinity). This is no more difficult than for the individual pursuit. It is most important, however, that you add suggestions about co-ordinating and relating to other players. Then see this: see and feel some combined move, culminating in a goal. Where the coach has gone over fixed moves in some formation, picture these clearly and see them being executed, with each player doing exactly the right thing, and not just yourself.

In group sports, lack of confidence is more difficult to deal with. The best method in using hypnosis for this is for the whole team to be hypnotized by a hypnotist, prior to a number of matches, until there is a return of confidence. During such sessions, suggestions, instilling success, should be frequent. Belief that you can win is more than half way to winning.

In the case of individual performances in sport, there is undoubtedly more potential for the use of self-hypnosis and imagery. Once you have recognized that sport must be played with both sides of the brain, then the aim is to cultivate the use of the right brain as well as the left.

# 11
# SELF-HYPNOSIS AND EDUCATION

Education is a vast topic and my intention here, therefore, is very selective. We shall assume that you have now achieved success in hypnotizing yourself. Having done this, I wish to point out uses to which it can be put in an educational context. This chapter is directed mostly at teachers and students, but it is also useful to anyone who is involved in some form of learning – whether it be a job, a foreign language or something done at night school for interest and pleasure. The aim is simple: How to involve your right brain more in the learning process.

We have already pointed out that the left brain is the one involved in words, logic and reasoning; while the right brain is involved in imagination, creativity and synthesis. The difficulty faced by Western man is not knowing how to incorporate the right brain consciously in the learning process. For this reason, man's potential is great while his actual performance is quite poor. There is a great tendency to 'set our sights too low'. This partly arises from the fact that our left brains are overloaded and this tends to happen fairly readily, because our left brain works in a *linear* fashion. If you were asked to make a summary of this chapter, in all probability, you would set out headings and sub-headings; you would begin at the top of the page and work downwards. You might say that is the 'natural' way to do it. But no. It is 'natural' for the left brain, but not for the right. The right brain is interested in interconnections.

Turn now to the end of this chapter and look over the 'mental map' given there, which the author used as the basis for this chapter. It is very easy from this, to 'picture' the chapter with one look. The information supplied in this form tends to be absorbed more by the right brain. It is set out, suitable for absorption by the right brain. This *non-linear* presentation of information in the form of 'mental maps' has been highlighted particularly by Tony Buzan and P. Russell, whose books are listed in the references. The advantage of such 'maps' probably rests on the holographic nature of the mind, which we outlined in Chapter 8.

The only point I am trying to demonstrate is that we only feel we cannot deal with the large inflow of information and learning, because we do not utilize the right brain fully enough. Of course, you can cultivate right brain learning techniques, such as the 'mental maps' just referred to, without the need of hypnosis. What I wish to do in this chapter, is concentrate on using self-hypnosis as a means of activating the right brain. It is certainly an efficient way to do it.

## Learning and Recall

There is overwhelming evidence that our minds store absolutely everything that our senses pick up over the whole of our life span. Let us, then, assume that this is true. Then two issues follow immediately. The incoming information is shared between the left and right hemispheres of the brain. Suppose, for instance, you are talking to someone. The verbal part is being processed by the left brain, while the right brain processes gestures and intonations, etc. We respond very much to gestures, but not at the conscious level. This is quite understandable from our present analysis. Gestures are a right brain function, and so tend to be picked up by our unconscious mind. This is why you can 'feel' that someone means something quite different from what they are saying. Your right and left brains are picking up conflicting information. The second issue concerns the fact that to remember something is to bring it back into conscious awareness. Memory is concerned with the recall of information that exists in the mind.

We can conclude briefly from what has been said. Learning is both a right brain and a left brain operation, even though, in the past, it has been dominated by the idea of being solely a left brain operation. Second, recall means to bring the information back into conscious awareness, i.e. allow the information back into the left brain. To facilitate recall, we need to create a situation which allows information to flow more readily from the right brain into the left brain. Self-hypnosis can be useful, both in learning and in recall.

Let me first take recall. The memory functions best when it is relaxed. The relaxation exercises supplied in Chapter 6 should, if you are carrying them out, have the added benefit of improving your memory. You will find that those things you wish to recall come more readily into your consciousness. This has probably something to do with the corpus callosum and the fact that, under hypnosis, you get practice at passing information between the two halves of the brain – and practice always makes things easier in the future.

If there is something particular and important for you to remember, then put yourself into a hypnotic state and begin to think about the topic – but do not consciously try to remember. Simply let the problem, in all its manifestations, 'mull over in your mind' and soon, the thing you particularly wish to remember will be passed into your left brain – into your conscious awareness. It often occurs, quite suddenly, like a revelation or 'bolt from the blue'. As we have remarked earlier, this is a natural feature of the mind. You do not need any specific suggestions for remembering, other than those to focus on the thing or situation. You could, however, give suggestions which will recreate, in your mind's eye, the situation when you first did or read the thing you wish to remember.

Let us take a simple, but effective illustration. Suppose you wish to remember a telephone number and, for some reason, you do not have access to the operator, or you do not know the address and it's a fairly common name. The circumstances are really not important. What you can do is hypnotize yourself and imagine a situation where you are ringing up the person.

Begin with your decision to do so, of going to the telephone and see yourself dialing the number. In all likelihood, the number will pop into your conscious awareness. If you have the number in a book, see yourself turning the page, picture the page clearly. Picturing the location of something on a page, as an aid to recall, is a very common practice. It can be made more effective when you are in a hypnotic state.

As an aid to learning, self-hypnosis can be used in a variety of ways. In Chapter 8, we showed how it could be used for solving a problem. The same procedure could be applied for preparing an essay. The aim, here, is to utilize both self-hypnosis and features of the right brain by means of mental maps. To give a simple illustration as to how the instructions can be formulated, suppose you are going to prepare an essay:

### Preparing an Essay

[Name], you are, in a moment, going to sit at your desk and make an outline for the essay you are about to do. You will arrange the material in the form of a mental map and you will put down all the relevant ideas, regardless of how they interconnect. If, however, you see interconnections, you will link them on the map. And you will find all this very easy and straightforward. The information will readily materialize in your consciousness and you will have no difficulty remembering all the relevant pieces of information. At this stage, however, your aim is to concentrate on the main ideas you wish to develop in your essay. And, as you carry out your 'mental map', an idea of how to structure your essay to good effect will also arise in your conscious awareness.

These suggestions can be adapted to your own style of preparation. But the essence is to prepare yourself for the task ahead. You have two choices open to you. You can either prepare the essay while still in a hypnotic state, or you can awaken yourself and then carry out the preparation. The wording should be changed slightly if you intend to do it in the waking state, to make the suggestions clearly post-hypnotic. In this instance, you should phrase it along the lines;

In a moment, when you awaken, you will prepare your essay. And when you are doing this you will ...

You can, if you so wish, write the essay while in a hypnotic state. There is no possibility that it will not make sense. You are not, as is the case with some drugs, incapable of reason. You will find that the ideas flow easily and quickly. If you do not wish to write it under hypnosis, give yourself a post-hypnotic suggestion that the ideas will flow easily and quickly and that you will remain relaxed. Combine it with the post-hypnotic, one-pointed attention instruction given later.

Investigations into reading, show that you achieve better comprehension and you remember more if you read fast. It is not my intention here to discuss speed reading, but when you have a great deal to read, say in preparation for an essay, it would be useful if you could use self-hypnosis – and you can. The instruction is a straightforward post-hypnotic suggestion, to be carried out when you awaken. In giving this instruction, we shall suppose you have put three hours aside for reading.

### Post-hypnotic Suggestion for Reading

When you awaken, [name], you will begin to read ... and you will find that you will read faster than usual and that you will be more able to comprehend what you read. And you will be able to do this because, as you read faster, the author's ideas and intentions will be made clearer more quickly, and so you will be able to follow more easily what the author is saying.

And while you read, you will be very calm and relaxed. Yes, [name], you will be very calm and relaxed. And because you are so calm and relaxed, you will be able to direct all your attention to what you are reading. And you will become very absorbed in your reading and you will find that you will have no difficulty in concentrating, no difficulty in following the argument, and you will be able to see exactly what the author is trying to say. And you will also be able to see, quite clearly, any shortcomings in the author's arguments.

Yes, [name], you will read quickly and easily. When you awaken, you will read ... quickly and easily, and throughout your reading you will not be distracted, and you will remain very relaxed so that you can apply all your concentration, all your awareness, to the task in hand.

It should be noted that this particular post-hypnotic suggestion can be used for any task where concentration is required. It could, for instance, be adapted to some typing that you have to do. Here you would suggest speed along with proficiency: and always a feeling of being very relaxed while carrying out the task.

Undoubtedly, time distortion is one of the major uses to which hypnosis can be put in the area of education. If you are very busy and must consider a number of books and articles in a given time, then it would be of inestimable value if you could expand that time. This applies to any learning situation. The basic idea is exactly the same as is described in Chapter 7. If used as a post-hypnotic suggestion, you simply repeat that time is going to go very very slowly and that you will have sufficient time to cover all of your work. That you will remain relaxed throughout and that your attention will not wander and that you will not be interested in excuses that will cause delays. Time distortion combined with one-pointed attention (dealt with in the next section), can be even more effective.

## Getting the Most Out of Your Day

This particular section could have gone virtually anywhere in Part II, but it is a more useful technique for the executive or the person involved in education. Some people seem more efficient than others. The question is: why? There are a number of reasons, but one is of special interest. Some people have, what I shall call, *one-pointed attention*. They have the ability to apply themselves to the task in hand and nothing else. When they turn to the next task, they apply themselves again, neither considering their previous task nor the one to come. By doing this, they usually get through more work in any specified time.

In this section, it is my intention to give a post-hypnotic suggestion which can be used each day and incorporates the idea of one-pointed attention. But first, it is necessary to develop a symbol to represent one-pointed attention. In doing this, the idea is to activate the right brain into co-operating in this endeavour. By formulating a symbol, your full awareness is brought to bear on the idea of one-pointedness. You can either devise a mental symbol or some action that typifies the idea of one-pointedness. In my own case, for instance, I bring

my arms up and bring my finger tips together and form a
point. It is clear that this conjures up, in a symbolic form, the
idea of one-pointedness.

Having decided on your symbol, your next task is to have a
rough plan of the day. This does not have to be specific, but if
there are things to be done that day, incorporate them into
your suggestions. The more specific you can be, the more
effective the suggestions are likely to be. Three basic themes
run through the instructions: (1) remaining relaxed all day; (2)
being able to concentrate; and (3) carrying out each task with
one-pointed attention. This is such a useful set of instructions
for the self-hypnotist that I shall give it in full.

**Post-hypnotic Suggestion Involving One-pointed Attention**
Today, [name], you are going to work quickly and efficiently.
This does not mean you are going to work every moment of the
day. No, it means that during those hours you intend to work,
you will work very efficiently indeed. (pause)
And, [name], you will work efficiently because you will be
relaxed all day. Yes, throughout the day you are going to
remain very calm and relaxed. And because you will be so calm
and relaxed throughout the day, so you will be able to apply
yourself to the job in hand. You will, [name], be able to
concentrate easier than ever before, because you are so
relaxed. Yes, [name], your concentration is going to be very
good and your mind is going to be crystal-clear. In fact, you are
going to find it easy to concentrate on whatever you are doing
throughout the whole day (pause).
And more than that, [name], you are going to approach each
task with one-pointed attention. Yes, you know that it is very
important for you to approach each task with one-pointed
attention. So you will *now* symbolize how you are going to
approach each new task. Yes, symbolize this one-pointedness
that you are going to do when you come to each new task.
(pause).
[Repeat, if necessary, but make sure you carry out the
symbolization. Keep repeating until this is achieved.]
Yes, [name], you are going to be very efficient today. You are
going to be very relaxed throughout the day and because you
are going to be so relaxed, you will be able to concentrate on

everything you do without any difficulty. And each job you undertake, you will approach it with one-pointed attention. Yes, you will concentrate on that job and that job alone. And so, because of all these reasons, you will work quickly and efficiently today.

[At this point, you should mention specifics. If some jobs are to be done before others, then list the order in which they should be carried out.]

And, [name], you are not going to be dragged away from your stated purpose unless it is important or has to be done. You will not find excuses for not doing the things which have to be done. For you will find no need to do this because you are concentrating very well and have one-pointed attention. You will be concerned only about performing the task in hand to the best of your ability.

And because you will be working well and efficiently, you will know that you cannot do more than what you are doing and so this too will give you a feeling of satisfaction.

And, [name], you will find that because you are so relaxed all day and free from tension, you will be very cheerful. You will look on the bright side of everything and, in this way, your day will also be an enjoyable one.

It is important to finish off with this idea of having an enjoyable day. You obviously do not wish to become a work machine. The idea is to be efficient during the hours you actually work. After using this post-hypnotic suggestion frequently, it can be shortened once a stimulus-response pattern is established. As you use this suggestion, you will find that your work performance rises considerably and yet you still have plenty of time for other pursuits. When you find this occurs, you will realize the great potential we all have, but have failed to achieve.

## Examinations

Examinations are a part of learning which we are not likely to do away with. Some people take them in their stride, but for many, they lead to periods of anxiety, insomnia and, in some cases, worse still. In most aspects of examinations, self-hypnosis can help.

Periods of relaxation and suggestions of self-confidence will remove quite a bit of tension. Suggestions for reading, preparing essays and general revision can be aided by suggestions, given earlier in this chapter. Performance, by means of post-hypnotic suggestions, can be improved and you can utilize time distortion very effectively in such a situation. Most of these suggestions have been dealt with in various chapters. Here I shall concentrate on two sets of instructions. One to deal with insomnia, which of course can be utilized at any time; and a second, to improve performance in the actual examinations. Both of these are post-hypnotic suggestions.

### Dealing with Insomnia

Tonight, [name], and any night you wish to sleep better, you will carry out the following suggestions. You will close your eyes and begin a progressive set of relaxation instructions. But on this occasion, and any occasion that you carry this out in bed, you will find that you will become so relaxed that you will very soon fall into a *natural* sleep. Yes, on these occasions, when you give yourself these instructions whilst lying in bed, you will, very soon, go into a natural sleep.

With each breath you take, you will become more tired and sleepy, naturally tired and sleepy. And, very soon, you will pass into a natural sleep.

You can embellish this a bit. Try, however, to see yourself in bed and see yourself responding and falling asleep. If you have carried out the relaxation suggestions repeatedly, you will have already created a stimulus-response pattern and so, when you do this at night in bed, you very soon enter natural sleep. If you find this does not happen, because you are particularly anxious, then a much stronger visual image is called for. Be extremely imaginative and have all the suggestions directed at the one theme – you falling into a profound sleep. Again, the aim is not to leave this until you actually have insomnia, but to practise it whenever you feel like it, so that when the need does arise, you have already established a suitable stimulus-response mechanism.

Let us now turn to the period prior to an examination. We achieve our greatest success in examinations if we can accomplish three things: (1) relaxation, (2) improved concentration and one-pointedness, and (3) better recall of information. The purpose of the following post-hypnotic suggestion is to improve all of these *and* to suggest time expansion along with over all self-confidence. It is important to incorporate all these features because they will reinforce one another.

### Examination Performance

Tomorrow you will be sitting your exam in ... Tonight you will sleep very soundly and very well so that you will awaken refreshed for the examination.

And, [name], when you sit down in your seat in the examination room, that is a signal for you to relax, yes, you *will* relax even while you are doing your paper. You will remain very relaxed throughout the whole period.

And because you are relaxed, you will be able to concentrate that much better. Yes, [name], you will find no difficulty in concentrating. And when you begin each question, you will approach it with one-pointed attention. Yes, you are *now* symbolizing the one-pointed attention that you will have during your examination (pause).

And, [name], the relaxation plus the one-pointedness will enable you to recall all the necessary information for that question – easily, very easily, indeed. And this is going to happen for each question you choose to answer. And you are confident and know that you are going to do a good paper. You will feel relaxed and confident tomorrow when you are doing your paper. And this relaxation and confidence will ensure that you do write a good paper.

And part of the reason for this confidence is the knowledge that you will be very relaxed and will be able to remember all the relevant material. But, more than that, [name], you will find that time will seem to go very, very slowly and that you will have plenty of time to write out all that you know about the questions being asked. Yes, each half hour is going to seem to you as if it is an hour and that you will be able to do in half an hour what would normally take you an hour or more.

You should picture yourself in the examination carrying out these instructions. See yourself, confident and answering the questions easily, quickly and fully.

## Learning a Language

This is a vast subject, so we shall be brief. Many people, at one stage or another, learn a language and some, more than one. Self-hypnosis can aid the learning process considerably. The most obvious way to listen to a language when you are learning it, is while you are in a hypnotic state. In this way, it passes more readily into the unconscious mind. This means that if you have a record or cassette with the language on, then play this frequently and try as often as possible to do it in a relaxed hypnotic state. You may almost pay it no attention, but you will still find that you remember more than usual.

Individual words and phrases can also be learned in this way. Although there are many teaching aids used in learning languages, if they are *combined* with hypnosis your learning can progress quicker and easier. One method to employ is a variant of sleep learning. The most direct way is to simply have the words on a tape and have the tape come on during the night – by having your cassette plugged into a time-switch. But this too can be made more effective if the whole thing is done as a hypnotic routine. In other words, have first a brief induction and deepening, then secondly, instructions that you will learn the language quickly and easily and very fluently. Visualize this and the feeling of being fluent. Have a section of the tape well marked, e.g. 100-200 on the counter, for new words or phrases. This can, periodically, be wiped and replaced, with the remainder left undisturbed. When you first play such tapes, you will probably find you awaken, but after three nights or so you become accustomed to the noise, and so you probably will not awaken thereafter. The tape must, however, be played very low at a hardly audible level. The unconscious mind can still pick it up and, this way, you will not repeatedly awaken.

## Other Educational Uses

There are a large variety of other uses to which self-hypnosis can be put in the area of education. Some obvious situations are:

| | |
|---|---|
| Typing and shorthand | Debating |
| One-off speeches | Drama |
| Seminars and tutorials | Music |
| Public lectures | |

In all cases, the situations resemble those we have dealt with in previous sections. Its use in drama and music can be very significant. The reason is because these arts already utilize right brain attributes. Under self-hypnosis, they can be considerably enhanced. In music, you can learn to feel the piece and so allow it to become more meaningful. In practice sessions, you can get your fingers to move quicker and more spontaneously. Visualization can be utilized to very good effect.

Drama in particular can benefit from the use of self-hypnosis. A feel for the part or the play can be enhanced. You can act out, under hypnosis, your part more effectively and can reduce the feeling of self-consciousness. It is no surprise to find that actors are very good hypnotic subjects.

The secret is to be inventive and imaginative in your suggestions and keep trying alternatives until you become satisfied. Direct them specifically at the task in hand, and above all, ensure that a well defined stimulus-response mechanism is established.

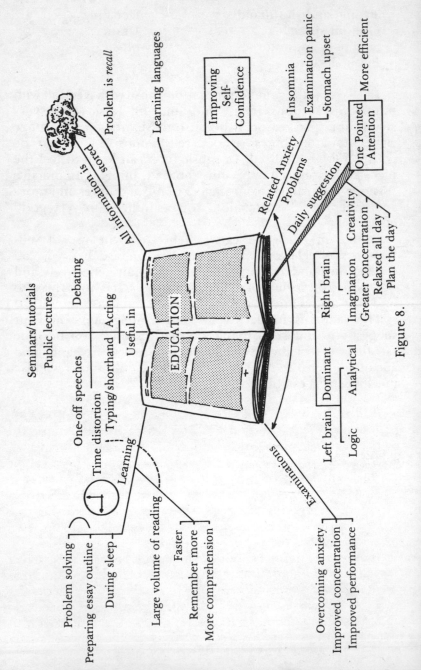

Figure 8.

# 12
# CONCLUSION

In Part I, the induction of self-hypnosis and how to achieve the full effect of this technique was considered. In doing this, I emphasized that the features of hypnosis are connected with characteristics of the right-left brain division. Both sides of the brain are involved in hypnosis, but the induction routine, along with deepening, is to lessen the influence of the left brain and so prevent the reality principle placing constraints on the operation of the pleasure principle. In Part II, I concentrated on the uses to which self-hypnosis can be put in non-medical situations. This concentration seems justified because the literature on hypnosis has, for too long, dealt almost exclusively with medical uses. The reason for this has been because the professional hypnotists have been largely doctors. There is no reason why this should be so. As we have argued in this book, hypnotic phenomena are common in many experiences that we all have. Why should we not use these abilities to our own benefit, and so reach our full potential?

Self-hypnosis can be induced and experienced in about half an hour. This should not, however, give the impression that half an hour is long enough to experience all the experiences we have discussed in this book. It can be achieved quickly, at least by some people, because we all have experienced it in one form or another before. But this is not the same as having mastery of the technique. We can all drive a car in our first lesson, but no-one would suggest you are ready to go-it-alone, and have mastery of driving. Self-hypnosis is no different. It must be practised to attain any degree of proficiency in using it.

Perhaps, like many other people, you have already been to a hypnotist in order to stop smoking, for instance. What I find unjustified is the expectation that, after one session, lasting, say, one hour, you will automatically succeed in your endeavour. Every time you put a cigarette in your mouth and associate it with pleasure, you create and reinforce a stimulus-response. Just imagine the hundreds, if not thousands, of times you do this. To then expect, with one (or even five) sessions, to break this stimulus-response is asking a lot – one might even say a miracle. Suppose, as is likely, that after a day or so you are smoking once again; to conclude from this that hypnosis, heterohypnosis or self-hypnosis, is of no use is positively unfair. You are asking of the technique far more than it can deliver. It *can* be most useful, but it cannot deal with all those problems normal medicine cannot deal with.

What I have attempted to do in this book is to explain what hypnosis is, how it works and how it can be used by yourself on yourself. It is no panacea and no miracle cure. At the same time, it is not mysterious. The mystery arises only from Western man's insistence on using his left brain and assuming all existence, all usefulness, is that which can be processed ('understood') by the left brain. We simply do not know how to stimulate the right brain and, more significantly, we do not know how to utilize the principles on which the right brain works. We all dream, and we do so every night of our lives, and yet we know so little about dreams and their function. We know more about mathematics and logic (a left brain function) than we do about dreams (a right brain function). Yet dreams are older than mathematics and logic and most of us dream more frequently than we carry out mathematics or need logic. I am not undermining the benefits of left brain abilities; I am simply pointing out that such dominance has led to wasted potential in human creativity and endeavour. One, and only one aspect of this, is the inability to use the technique of hypnosis.

The non-medical uses to which self-hypnosis can be put, which were discussed in Part II, are really only the tip of the iceberg. The chapters on sport and education, in particular, could each fill a book. But, as yet, little work has been done in these areas. Research, however, very often follows practice. People can use self-hypnosis in both of these areas to great effect. Once it is used, we will, no doubt, find experimenters and researchers explaining why it works.

A major emphasis in this work has been the role of the imagination. This has been, in my view, the most underrated human facility. In fact, Western man positively stops its development from a very early age – out go the fairies and the child's hallucinations. If a child is told to stop hallucinating enough times (which does not have to be a great number of times), then he will stop doing it and will very soon lose the ability to fantasize.

Let me finally recall H. G. Wells' story of the sighted man who lived in the village of the blind. The man who could see was arguing that the blind villagers were not perceiving reality as it 'really' was. In turn, they thought he was demented. What is reality? Let us suppose the left brain dominated man fell into a village of right brain dominated beings. How would they communicate? Which, if any, would be the 'true' reality?

Self-hypnosis will give you a new perspective on 'reality' and allow you to reach your full potential. Do we not all deserve the knowledge to reach the limits of our abilities?

# FURTHER READING

Bentov I. *Stalking the Wild Pendulum*. Fontana, 1979.

Blakeslee T.R. *The Right Brain*. The Macmillan Press Ltd., 1980.

Bloomfield H.H. et al. *T.M.* Allen and Unwin, 1976.

Brazier M.A.B. *The Analysis of Brain Waves*. Scientific America, 1962.

Buzan T. *Make the Most of Your Mind*. Pan Books, 1981.

Buzan T. *Use Your Head*. B.B.C. Publications, 1982.

Gallwey T.W. *The Inner Game of Tennis*. Cape, 1975.

Gallwey T.W. and Kriegal B. *Inner Skiing*. New York: Random House, 1977.

Gazzaniga M.S. *The Split Brain*. Scientific America, 1967.

Hartland J. *Medical and Dental Hypnosis and its Clinical Applications*. London. Balliere Tindall, 2nd ed. 1971.

Jacobson E. *You Must Relax*. Unwin, 1980.

Kleitman N. *Patterns of Dreaming*. Scientific America, 1960.

Ornstein R.E. *The Psychology of Consciousness*. Penguin, 1986.

Peale N.V. *The Power of Positive Thinking*. Ulverscroft, 1986.

Russell Peter *The Brain Book*. Routledge, 1980.

Schreiber F.R. *Sybil*. Penguin Books, 1975.

Sizemore C.C. and Pittillo E.S. *Eve*. New York, 1983.

# INDEX